12Y $1·49C

WIDOW

WIDOW

by Lynn Caine

WILLIAM MORROW & COMPANY, INC.
NEW YORK 1974

Book design by Helen Roberts

Printed in the United States of America.

6 7 8 9 10   77 76 75 74

Library of Congress Cataloging in Publication Data

Caine, Lynn.
    Widow.

    1. Bereavement—Personal narratives.   2. Widows.
I. Title.
BF575.G7C34   155.9'37   73-23124
ISBN 0-688-02850-0

To Buffy and Jon

Contents

Contents

Life must go on
And the dead be forgotten;
Life must go on,
Though good men die.

Anne, eat your breakfast;
Dan, take your medicine;
Life must go on;
I forget just why.

—*Edna St. Vincent Millay*

Introduction

After my husband died, I felt like one of those spi-
raled shells washed up on the beach. Poke a straw
through the twisting tunnel, around and around,
and there is nothing there. No flesh. No life. Whatever lived there is dried up and gone.

Our society is set up so that most women lose
their identities when their husbands die. Marriage
is a symbiotic relationship for most of us. We draw
our identities from our husbands. We add ourselves
to our men, pour ourselves into them and their lives.
We exist in their reflection. And then . . . ? If
they die . . . ? What is left? It's wrenching enough
to lose the man who is your lover, your companion,
your best friend, the father of your children, without losing yourself as well.

Death parts women from their loves more
often and earlier than it does men. One out of

every six women in this country over the age of twenty-one is a widow. And the statistics collected by the Bureau of the Census show that women are becoming widows at younger and younger ages. The Darby-and-Joan idyll, that blissful growing-old-together, is rare, rarer, rarest. For women, that is. Men have it better. More than 70 percent of men over sixty-five are married, compared to 30 percent of the women.

And that's the reason for this book. If wives have to face widowhood, and it seems that the great majority of them must, then women must be prepared for life after marriage ends. I'm not a writer and I'm particularly sensitive about this fact since my job as publicity manager at Little, Brown involves working with writers every day. But I have experiences and feelings as a widow that I want to share. They may help other widows survive as persons, knowing who they are, instead of slamming head-on into an identity crisis on top of their grief, their hurt, their rage—all the cataclysmic emotions of bereavement that leave even the strongest psyche tattered.

Enough. Let me tell you how it was.

Part One

THE DYING

1

When Love's Eye Turns Cold

My husband thought he would live forever. He knew better, of course, but that's the way he felt. Martin had been badly wounded in World War II. His plane had been shot down, half the crew was killed and Martin had shrapnel in his head and nearly lost a leg. He eventually came home after three years in an army hospital with a metal plate in his head and the Silver Star for gallantry in action in his pocket. He was a hero. And he was convinced that he would live forever, since he had cheated death once.

I asked him once how he felt when he was being prepared for the operation to put the metal plate in his head, a delicate procedure that required hours with only a local anesthetic. "Were you scared you might die?" I asked.

"No," Martin said. "I wasn't scared, but when I realized I might die, my first reaction was, 'My God, I won't be able to listen to Mozart anymore.'"

We had what I considered an unbelievably

satisfying marriage. We both worked very hard. He had his law practice and I had my job in publishing. We had each other and our children, Buffy, our daughter, and Jonny, our son. We considered ourselves a very special couple. And the life we led suited us perfectly. It was full of children, music, laughter and talk. Nights, after the children had been tucked in, Martin and I would sit and talk or listen to music until after midnight. I think that is what I miss most now—the talk, those long evenings. Martin was not only my husband and lover, he was my best friend.

Not that our life was all that serene. It wasn't. There were times when we fought like cats and dogs. Nor was either of us perfect.

Martin used to get angry at me—or say he was —for being mean and nasty to people I didn't like.

"Why can't you accept people?" he'd scold.

But then I would overhear him on the telephone an hour later saying fondly, "You know what Lynn said about so and so?" And he would repeat my latest crack and chuckle.

As for Martin. He was rotten in the morning. Grouchy and cranky. And he spent hours and hours at his bridge club. That was something that always irritated me since I didn't play bridge, and brought me to the boiling point periodically.

But if I had been asked five years ago to enumerate his faults, hypochondria would have topped the list. He was a chronic complainer. He had gout. He suffered from headaches. He had odd pains and twinges. He had indigestion. He had trouble sleeping. I got used to hearing him complain. I'd just say to myself, "Oh, Christ! There he goes again!" I never took it seriously, mostly because I knew that Harold, his doctor and his best friend since college days, checked him over every few months as painstakingly as NASA checks out a space launch.

Then I started to worry. I don't know what triggered it, but it was there, a kind of free-floating, nagging uneasiness. I remember calling Harold one day and telling him I was concerned about Martin and thought he should get a physical. Harold was very comforting and said, "Don't worry. Martin's going to outlive us all."

That made me feel better for a while, but then the worries came back. Instead of Martin's usual irritable resentment of physical discomfort, there was now a dark undercurrent of urgency, of fear in his complaints. And he was more controlled, somewhat more reticent than before. It was only the slightest degree of change, but, like an animal, I sensed danger.

Soon there was something tangible to worry about. Martin developed rectal bleeding. He rushed off to Harold. Examination showed a polyp, a rectal polyp like a cherry on a stem. These polyps were almost always benign, Harold said. But the bleeding continued. Martin's complaints diminished. I suddenly became distracted by worry.

I urged him to see another doctor. "You shouldn't be feeling this way all the time," I said. "Maybe Harold is missing something."

"No." Martin was convinced that Harold knew exactly what he was doing.

Then, one October afternoon, Martin and Jonny were wrestling on the living room rug. Suddenly Martin had a terrible pain in his chest. We rushed to the doctor's office. The X ray showed a cracked rib. I was alarmed. Eight-year-old Jonny could no more have cracked Martin's rib than I could have torn a telephone book in two. I had a terrible nightmare that night—all Martin's bones were crumbling. My worries doubled, tripled. But I kept telling myself I was being foolish. Martin had an excellent doctor, who was most attentive. And anyone can crack a rib. It was just some freak kind of stress.

A few weeks later, Martin had to go to Arizona on business. When he came home, there was something different about him. Something had happened. Martin was strange, but there was nothing I could put a finger on. He was his familiar self, playing with Jonny, teasing little Buffy, whom he adored, listening to my stories about authors and their vagaries. Everything was the same. But everything was different.

Months later, he told me that during that trip he learned he had cancer. He hadn't gone to a doctor or anything like that. "I had these drenching sweats at night," he told me. "And I'd read enough to know what they meant." * (Martin was a medicine buff. He had always devoured anything on the subject from Merck's Manual to the AMA Journal.) But he

* Doctors have told me that Martin was mistaken. A person who wakes up all sweaty in the middle of the night should not jump to the conclusion that he or she has cancer. Sweating is not an indication of cancer. However, if heavy sweating continues for several nights, it may be symptomatic of some disease process and one should consult a doctor.

didn't say a word about his knowledge or fear at the time. Not to me, at any rate.

When I look back, it seems as if we were living in a kind of fearful vacuum. There was a sense of doom just around the corner. But we didn't talk about it. Martin would complain. I would worry. He would go to the doctor. There would be no change. The weeks went by. The months went by. Our lives continued.

Then there was a horrible night. In February. It was Valentine's Day and we were going to a marvelous party. The host was wealthy and he had arranged an evening of chamber music, harking back to the bygone gilded age of the music patron. We were both looking forward to the gala evening.

It was terrible. It is stomach-wrenching even to think about it three years later.

As we were getting dressed, I looked at Martin. There are times when love's eye turns cold and you suddenly see a beloved person as if he were a stranger. I looked up in the mirror as I was putting on my makeup and watched Martin. He was absorbed in knotting his tie, completely oblivious of my inspection. And I was shocked. Shocked? Scared out of my wits. Martin looked like death.

To me, that was when the dying began. He had a grayness in his face that had nothing to do with fatigue. My beloved husband had the mark of death. I had seen it before. A dear friend of mine had died of leukemia and he had had the same look.

I didn't say anything. I couldn't say anything. How do you tell the man you love, "I think you're dying. You look like death to me."

WIDOW

We went to the party. I felt cold. It was a gray, raw, February night, but my cold was inside.

I had just started talking with a group of people when a woman barged into the conversation.

"Don't you know cigarettes cause cancer?" she asked self-righteously. "And you have two beautiful children. How can you risk leaving them without a mother?"

I had a great sense of impending disaster. Neither Martin nor I had ever said the word "cancer" out loud, but I kept remembering my friend who had died of leukemia and inside I was shivering with the foreknowledge of catastrophe. When that silly woman said "cancer," I tore into her. I told her to go away. I grabbed her little beaded handbag and opened it up. I pulled out her gold pillbox and sneered, "How can you bug people about cigarettes when you take downers?"

Our host was in a dither. He put what was supposed to be a soothing hand on my arm and asked, "What are you doing to my guest, Lynn?"

I knew people don't make scenes at parties. And I knew I was making a dreadful scene. All the fears, all the worry, all the rage that I'd been holding in came ripping out of me. That poor woman didn't have a chance.

And Martin? Dear Martin took it in his stride. He knew my reactions to panic.

What I'm beginning to realize is that we weren't really involved in anything that evening except ourselves. I was coming to terms with the realization that Martin was dying. And Martin, although we never once discussed this awful evening, knew it.

I knew that he knew what demon was riding me that night. I knew. He knew. He knew that I knew. I knew that he knew that I knew. And we didn't say a word to each other.

It was so strange. It was as if our emotional wiring had gone awry and all communications had to be extrasensory. The knowledge was too wounding, too burning, too enormously devastating to touch with words or even looks.

2

Prognosis Zero

Martin's rectal bleeding was getting worse and he was having more pain. His doctor, who was also his best friend, decided that it was time to operate. Harold was on the staff of a hospital in New Jersey and Martin took the bus over there one afternoon, very matter-of-factly. I would have gone with him, but this was the peak of my work year, the week of the National Book Awards. I was juggling a hundred and one chores—press releases, party arrangements, authors' emergencies. And more than that, I had this superstitious feeling that if I didn't go it wouldn't be real.

So Martin went to the hospital alone one cold March day. Not that that's any great tragedy. Once you sign in, the aides and nurses and interns swarm all over you with enemas and shaving and physicals and X rays, so there is no place or role for a devoted wife. The day of the operation itself, I was at the Hotel Biltmore. There was a National Book Awards panel on communications. One of the panelists was an Atlantic-Little, Brown author, Nicholas Johnson, then FCC commissioner. And it was important that I be on hand.

Just as it got under way, the telephone rang. It was for me. We were in the Biltmore's Bowman Room, one of those enormous party and meeting rooms. The call caused a certain amount of disturbance, and one of the NBA publicity women bustled up to me and requested testily, "Lynn, would you please arrange to get your personal telephone calls elsewhere."

I didn't answer her. She didn't know what this call meant. (And when she learned later, she was terribly contrite.) I opened my handbag and took out a Librium. I swallowed with difficulty. My mouth was dry. And then, only then, did I allow myself to pick up the receiver and say, "Lynn Caine speaking."

It was my office. They had a message. "Call your doctor," the secretary told me. I called Harold.

"We opened Martin up and it stinks," he said bluntly. "He's riddled with cancer. It has gone through his colon, to his liver."

Harold did everything he could, medically and personally. He had already alerted his wife. "Vivian is on her way to New York to pick you up," he told me. "We want you to come spend the night with us."

I made the necessary explanations to my colleagues. I was completely dry-eyed and more or less self-possessed. But it was just the beginning of the big act. I didn't really know what I was doing. I only knew that I had to maintain control.

Vivian picked me up, just as Harold had promised. She had thoughtfully arranged to have logs crackling away in the fireplace when we arrived. I huddled close to the fire, feeling that I would never be warm again.

I told Harold that I felt as if someone had just kicked me in the stomach with a big iron boot. Harold said, "Someone did."

It was a weird kind of in-between feeling. I didn't know what to do. I don't think I could have done anything.

Harold had told Martin the truth just as he told me.

"Am I going to make it?" Martin asked.

Harold had to tell him, "No, Martin, you aren't."

I was allowed to see him the next morning. I remember all the terrible tubes in his nose, in his arm, everywhere. But he had control of himself. Martin had the strongest will of anyone I ever knew. He had willed himself to recover from his war wounds. Now his will would not permit a single moment of weakness.

"I'm going to die, darling," he said. "I'm going to die. The prognosis is zero. And it's going to be harder on you than on me."

He had thought everything out. "I don't want a funeral," he instructed me. "I want to be cremated. And I don't know how much time we have left together. But let's do something nice, huh? Let's do all the things we care about."

I nodded and I tried to smile. "We will, darling," I promised. "We will." And we did.

3

Telling the Children

Martin accepted the fact that he was going to die. Almost. He was a gambler.

"I beat a rap once before that I wasn't supposed to," he reminded me. And there was one corner of his mind in which he was not accepting for a moment that he could die. That's not so unusual. Most of us find it impossible to accept our mortality. What made Martin different was his determination.

Martin believed that the finest human quality was the exercised will, the exercise of mind. He could do almost anything he made up his mind to do. Whatever he decided to do, he did. No matter how difficult it was.

He now directed all his energies toward living. As soon as he could, he went to a health spa in Florida to soak up the sun and regain the energy and strength drained from him by the operation. He very much wanted me to go with him. But I wouldn't. I couldn't.

Here was where the difference between the

living and the dying began to make itself felt. I was afraid. I was afraid to leave the children. They had been upset when Martin was in the hospital. The whole winter had been a tense and nervous season. Jonny and Buffy needed all the love and stability I could give them. This was no time for me to run off and leave them alone with the house-keeper.

But there was more to it than concern for the children. Instinctively I sensed that I needed time to absorb the fact that Martin was going to die. Going to die. That my fears were reality. I believed the prognosis. I didn't think Martin had a prayer of a chance. And I couldn't bear to see him gambling on life. I couldn't bear to watch him go through the whole routine of building himself up. I just couldn't bear it. Because I wouldn't permit myself denial at any point. I had lived with gray fear for too many long nights before the surgical confirmation. I knew. I just had to have time to come to terms with my knowledge.

On top of that, for the first time, I was afraid of jeopardizing my job. I had no idea what our financial situation was. We lived very comfortably —ate, drank, traveled, did everything we wanted. But I suddenly felt tremendously insecure. I was frightened that I might lose my job if I didn't show up every day. That was the beginning of the finan-cial anxieties that still haunt me.

There were other fears, too. I remember that when Martin was in Florida I felt like a lost child, a little girl wandering around this enormous office building on East Forty-second Street. "What am I doing with two children?" I would ask myself. "I can't even take care of myself." I wouldn't have felt that way before I was married. But then I didn't have children.

Before Martin left for Florida we told the children. Death isn't real to a small child. I've always had cats and Buffy and Jon had the usual quota of city pets—goldfish, turtles and immensely fecund gerbils—and we held little ceremonies when one died. Once we had a duck named Stanley. I really hated that duck. He was so messy. But there he was waddling around the apartment until he was hit by some duck disease. This time the children were terribly concerned. I remember Martin holding Stanley, still a duckling handful of fluff, and saying that he would take him to the animal hospital. And then Stanley suddenly died. The children understood his death, I think.

Now we talked about how to tell them and what to tell them. Martin said, "I want to do it." And I was relieved. How can you tell a four-year-old girl and an eight-year-old boy that their daddy is going to die and leave them? We decided that the only right way was to tell them the truth. The truth, we hoped, would protect them from any fearful fantasies that might besiege them. The truth was as bad as it could get.

Martin called the children into the living room. He was sitting in his rocking chair (and as I write this I feel guilty because I never got him the tie-on cushion for the back of the chair that he kept asking me for). I was on our long blue sofa holding Buffy on my lap, and Jonny was sitting beside me.

"I have a very serious disease," he said. "They discovered it in the hospital. It is called cancer. There is no cure for it. But a team of doctors is doing everything they can to help me. I'll be in and out of the hospital a lot, but I'll be home as often as I can to be with you."

There was dead silence. I'm not sure Buffy understood what Martin was saying. Jonny sat there, quite still, without his usual little-boy fidgeting.

I turned to him. "Is there anything you want to ask?" He shook his head.

Buffy and Jonny were faced with two stoics, me and Martin. Martin had always prided himself on his control, and that included control of his emotions. And I always took my cues from Martin. What he did, I did. And if he admired people who controlled their emotions, I controlled my emotions.

That night in bed, we discussed the afternoon and how the children had taken the news. We agreed that we had handled it just right. Martin had been straight, honest, true. We were also aware of a child's concept of time. You just don't talk about time beyond tomorrow. That night, we agreed we had said enough and not too much. And the children were tough. They'd be all right.

But today, if I had a chance to do it over again, oh, I would have played that scene so differently. I would have played it for the truth, the real emotional truth. Now I know what dangers there are in the cool, rational approach.

We believed in truth, but didn't once say the words "death" or "die" to Buffy and Jonny. We left the children with hope. Was this fair? Was this right? We were demanding that the children role-play right along with us. For Martin and I were into role playing with a vengeance although we would have denied it—and been honest in our denials. Our role from now on was gallantry in the face of death. And if God hands out Silver Stars, Martin should have one for his last gallant battle—even though he lost.

We not only balked at telling the children the facts, we failed to tell them the emotions. They had to learn that one can be bitter, one can rage and yet one cannot stand up against death. It conquers. But it need not conquer the living if they understand. If they know how to look down that gun barrel. We didn't know that, so how could we tell the children.

If I had been able to burst into wild tears when Martin told them, it would have done us all a lot of good. They probably would have cried, too, and we would all have been sobbing away. Martin and I would have been able to cry and to say, "We hate it a lot. It's a bum rap." But all my energies, then and later, were exerted in holding myself together. I always had this Humpty Dumpty fantasy that if I were ever to allow myself to crack, no one, not "all the King's men" could ever put me back together again. I'm beginning to learn how wrong I was. Emotions can strengthen you, not splinter you. To express emotions is healthier than to repress them.

So if I were given a chance to tell the children again, I would have encouraged them to cry. I would have worked hard to get them to ask questions, to talk about Daddy's illness. I would have tried to help them understand the truth. But I wasn't able to do it then.

When I was a little girl, my favorite story—the one I read over and over—was the story of the Little Spartan, the boy with the fox gnawing away at his innards who never betrayed his agony. I identified totally with that story. And even as an adult somewhere inside me I was still that nine-year-old girl trying so hard to be a Little Spartan.

I've seldom been able to cry. Not even when my father died, very shortly before Jonny was born. I told my obstetrician and he asked "Have you cried?"

"I can't," I said.

"I wish you could. It would be better for you," he said. Then he told me how when his father died, he couldn't cry either, but had had a bad reaction a year after. I forgot about it, but I remember leaving my office late, a year later. It was a beautiful night. There was a moon. I was looking forward to a drink and supper with Martin. Suddenly, I burst into tears on the street.

I don't know what kicked off the flood. But I sobbed and sobbed. It all swept over me. "My daddy is dead," I cried with my face to the wall of a building.

I still haven't been able to cry for Martin.

With emotional hindsight, I think there were some good things we did about telling the children. First of all, we told them. And no matter how we flubbed it, how evasive we were about the fact of death, they knew. They had something to start reacting to.

Evasive as I now think we were, many people were shocked by our directness. But, as Martin said,

"What are we expected to tell them? That Daddy is going away on a skillion business trips? No, we owe it to them to tell them that I am sick and I will be in the hospital a lot of the time."

The other thing I'm proud of was Martin's use of the phrase "a team of doctors." He had worked this out carefully. The children loved Harold. They called him Uncle Harold. And Martin expected that Harold, as his best friend, would play a part in our future after he died. He didn't want the children to be angry at Harold or blame him for their father's death. So he used the phrase "a team of doctors."

I still don't know what the right way is to tell children that their father is going to die. But I do know that it is not smooth, not clinical, not dispassionate. That lack of emotion is in itself a kind of death.

We should *not* have allowed the children to react with the dead silence they did. And we should have picked up the conversation again, a few days later, when they had had a chance to let it all simmer in their heads. Casually. And again and again.

Did it warp the children? Hurt them irretrievably? I don't think so. Both Buffy and Jon have suffered in their own ways. They still do. It's hard to grow up without a father. But they are strong individuals and no one can get through life without loss and grief. But I do think we could have handled the telling and the knowing better for them—and for ourselves. In the end, Martin and I were the ones who suffered from our stoic control. And I most of all. I am the one who is alive.

4

The Best Summer of Our Lives

Martin and I set about making the most of the time we had left with great passion. What we wanted most of all were good friends, good music, good food and wine, a place in the country for the summer.

Martin had come back from Florida standing straight, tan, looking strong and healthy. We didn't know how much time we had left. We never thought we'd have a year. Actually we had fourteen months, but those were just calendar months. After the first month, every day was harder for Martin than the day before. And the last five or six months—you could not call them living. They were a gradual withdrawal, a grudging letting go. It was being weaned from hope. Martin had found life glorious and he never wanted to give it up.

Early on, there was a miraculous flare of hope. He had been taking an experimental drug and now there was a remission, so the report said. A significant remission. Martin was convinced that he had turned the tide, that he was going to win the war. We were elated. The next day, we were told it was a mistake. The radiologist had read the liver scan incorrectly. The disease was progressing. There was no remission. We never discussed the episode. It was too painful.

What we talked about most was how to spend our time. The most important thing was always the time—what to do with it, what to buy, what to eat. We bought everything we liked. We were absolutely self-indulgent. We just did not give a damn about money.

One June weekend we found our dream house in southern Vermont. It was simple, a white New England clapboard with green shutters set in sixty acres of Vermont hills and pastures on a little dirt road that wound off another dirt road. We were completely hidden and yet close to Marlboro and the music festival. There were wild flowers all around the house. It had a big sunny kitchen, a fireplace that we used on cool evenings and a shed with snowshoes hanging on the wall. It belonged to a Boston lawyer who used it as a ski house in the winter. Martin loved it and we rented it immediately. All that summer he would fantasize about buying it. He was always talking about what he would do if he owned it. It was the perfect house for us.

We rented a station wagon for our Vermont summer, and every weekend we drove up with a huge hamper full of steaks and lobster and salmon. Everything we liked to eat. Martin put together a superb wine cellar for the summer. I remember thinking that it was sacrilege to be drinking Mouton Cadet or Aloxe-Corton with steak and salad. But we did and we loved it. That is, we did it for a little while.

After the first few weeks, Martin would just pick at his food and throw up a lot. He was in pain. Most of the time he was miserable. He couldn't really eat. And he couldn't drink—not even a sip of his favorite wines. Yet we kept inviting our friends for weekends and we kept cooking enormous steaks and uncorking wonderful red wine. Both of us felt a great need to maintain the continuity of life, not to deviate except in this one area—the area of self-indulgence.

Martin had always wanted a cashmere sport jacket and now he had one made in a beautiful black and white herringbone weave. He bought a lot of expensive ties. I suppose he was trying to convince himself that he was going to live, that everything would be fine and he would wear his expensive new sport jacket for years.

Both of us bought and bought and bought. We bought a lot of records. A new phonograph. I bought a lot of machines. That was very odd, because I have no mechanical aptitude whatsoever. I have never been able to learn to drive. I bought a sewing machine, I who have never sewn on a button without grinding my teeth. I've never used it, never even put thread in it. I had some sort of thought that when this crazy extravagant time was over I'd have to retrench, and if I had a sewing machine I could make my own clothes, and Buffy's, too. For some unfathomable reason, I also bought a freezer. I think I was planning to change character as soon as Martin died. I had these fantasies of how I would watch the supermarket specials, buy food in quantity when it was in season and store all my bargains in my freezer. Mrs. Practical, the thrifty widow. Machines symbolized something that could help me after Martin died. I bought eight bed pillows one afternoon, pillows that I didn't need. I couldn't resist the idea of softness and comfort.

In August, I took my vacation and we looked forward to an uninterrupted few weeks of more music, more friends. For the first time in my life, I was really enjoying the country. I'm a city woman and I can't stand the green leaves, the bugs, the birds at dawn, all the things that turn nature-lovers on. But this summer I spent more time out of doors than ever in my life. My childhood freckles reappeared. Martin and I would go for walks. Everything was so fresh. It smelled so good. One evening we were walking along our little dirt road after dinner, holding hands, and Martin started singing. He had a terrible voice, but he loved to sing. I was almost overcome with joy. If he could sing, I knew he wasn't in pain. That's all I cared about then. I was very happy.

I keep coming back to the thought that it was the happiest summer of our marriage. Everything was so beautiful. And while it was all spoiled by Martin being so ill, at the same time we were happy. It's true. We were happy. It's hard to believe, and I can't understand it, particularly since it was an up and down summer. Harold had managed to get Martin into the National Institutes of Health cancer-research program in Baltimore. This meant that Martin was a guinea pig. He was an eager guinea pig, more than ready to try any drug, any treatment, do anything, let them put anything into him, in order to live. So the summer was punctuated with his trips to Baltimore for treatments. One day here. Four days there. We never knew how he would feel or how he would react.

My vacation that we'd looked forward to so much gradually turned into a horror as Martin's condition worsened. He had to leave and go to Baltimore in the middle of it. He was wracked with pain.

It was hard for me to endure the change in his looks, although he rarely mentioned it. And that was a switch, because Martin had always been very meticulous about his appearance. He had a full head of beautiful hair that had gone quite white in his forties. Chemotherapy makes your hair fall out, but Martin disregarded this, except to make a joke early on when it began coming out in his comb. He said, "Okay, that's the end. No more chemotherapy." No, his vanity was an extravagance, one that was easy for him to give up. The change in his looks was much harder on me than on him.

There were other changes, too. In contrast to the days before the cancer was discovered, Martin seldom complained now, although the pain was excruciating. He became emaciated and the eighteen-year-old son of friends told me he used to think of Martin as "the spider." His legs and arms were bone thin. All there was to him was his huge liver tumor that kept growing and growing. He couldn't button his trousers anymore, and for a fastidious man like

Martin, that was so awful. He couldn't tie his shoes. There were days in Vermont when he could barely stand because of the pain. I would help him to his big chair under the trees. I would look at him. That dear face. I hardly knew it. His eyes were sunken way back in his head.

And though Martin wanted our friends around, he was so torn and fatigued by pain that it often was an imposition on him and on them. Yet, on the whole, the presence of friends was a blessing. We had not hesitated for one moment to tell everyone we cared about that Martin was dying. Dying from cancer. We found it easy to speak the unspeakable to friends, although we had not been able to tell our children the truth. After the first few calls to family and our very dearest friends, the word got around. And the telephone kept ringing. This helped, just knowing we were surrounded by love and concern.

It was harder for our friends than for us. Cancer is a shocking word. It triggers all the sneaky, repressed fears of death and pain and disfigurement. I was enormously moved by the way our friends dismissed their own fears to come to our emotional support. Everyone was marvelous. We never felt alone. And while there were days that last summer when I worried that the mere presence of friends was draining Martin's last bits of energy and life, I knew that they also made his life bearable.

But there were days when he felt better, when he could walk and we explored the paths meandering through the woods. Sometimes we took the chil-

dren with us. There were good days when we
laughed a lot. Once when we were all together, I
remembered another golden summer day. It was
in Maine. Martin and I were walking with Jonny,
who was just two then, along a cart track that
wound through an apple orchard. Suddenly Jonny
looked up at a tree and seemed to see it for the first
time. He started laughing, and he laughed so hard
he fell down and had a marvelous time rolling
around on the ground.

"What is it, Jonny? What's so funny?" we
asked.

"Apu! Apu!" he gurgled and burst into laughter
again.

It finally dawned on us that Jonny had never
seen an apple except in a fruit bowl or in the bin
at the grocery store. Now here they were hanging
on trees. And that struck Jonny's funny bone. To
his two-year-old way of thinking, a tree was a crazy
place for an apple to be hanging.

I told the story all over again. Jonny loved it
and so did Buffy, who always liked to hear stories
about her big brother. Things like that made the
summer precious.

One afternoon, Martin said to me, "This is the
best summer of our lives." And he was right. It was
a last honeymoon, but it was better than a honeymoon. It was different, because this was all there
was. All there was going to be. There wasn't going
to be any more.

We made love for the last time that summer.
Ever since Martin had come back from Florida, our

lovemaking had had a particular sweetness. We knew there wasn't much more. And often, when it was over and we were lying together peacefully, I would suddenly experience such a turmoil of emotions that I didn't know how to manage them. I felt love, and the delicious sense of physical satisfaction, physical fatigue; I felt hate that the man who could make me feel this way was leaving me; I felt anxiety that it might be too much for him, fear that we might never do it again. And shame, shame for feeling this way. After all, I was healthy. Martin was dying. I knew he didn't want to die. How could I always be thinking of myself?

The last time we made love was a miniature representation of the whole summer—part wonder, part horror. It was good sex. It always was with Martin. He was a good lover. We were tender with each other, we were excited. And then Martin shouted and recoiled. I was scared. I didn't know what had happened. Had something terrible gone wrong? He had never had sudden pains with the cancer, but this . . . It turned out to be our cat. For the first time in her life she had jumped on the bed while we were making love and bitten Martin on his big toe.

It sounds funny, but it wasn't the least bit amusing. We had to dress and go to the hospital immediately so Martin could get a shot. His white cell count was so low that a bite was potentially deadly. That was the end of lovemaking, although we didn't realize it at the time.

By the end of the summer, Martin was quite withdrawn. He was constantly in pain. He had to spend more and more time in the hospital in Baltimore. And I was anxious to get back to the city. I was tired. I was full of conflicting emotions. I knew the good time was over.

5

The End of the Happily Ever After

Now the nightmare began. So much living left to do and so little time, so little strength. Yet I regret that we spent our miserable hoard of life and strength (for Martin's life was my life and my strength, too) so grudgingly. We were profligate with money, but with emotions, with reality, we were miserly. The tranquility of summer was lost. It would return occasionally, but evaporate almost immediately.

Now, instead of confronting our feelings, both of us were role-playing in a big way. The courageous couple. Here we are, this marvelous, attractive, gallant pair facing disaster—and aren't we wonderful? We would laugh at ourselves, but just the same we thought we were pretty great.

"Aren't we classy?" we'd laugh at the end of an evening with friends.

And Martin would warn, "Don't get too carried away with it."

But he was the one who was carried away. I

wanted to cry and scream and rage, but this was not my role. Mine was a reflection of Martin's. Martin was brave. Martin was fantastic. Everyone admired Martin. After his death, I received a letter from Francis Steegmuller, that most perceptive of writers and the only person who understood. "Martin's heroism," he wrote, "must have been very difficult for you." And, dear God, it was!

But I measured up. Months later when the condolence letters came spilling in, I got my applause. "You were such an inspiration to all of us as we watched and admired you," one colleague said. An editor wrote, "Your spirit spurred us all on." And another, "All of us hope we can conduct ourselves as magnificently as you did."

Courage and gallantry. That was all the world was supposed to see. Or wanted to see. People appreciate role-playing because it makes it easier for them. No one knows what to do with a tumultuous, angry, sobbing woman who is railing at the fates for taking her husband.

It would have been far better to face our terrors instead of pretending to rise above them, better to talk about our fears together and perhaps come to terms with them. But we talked less and less. We were no longer open with each other. Oh, we were occasionally, but those were blessed moments, and they were too rare. I never told Martin how angry I was with him for being so heroic and for casting me as a heroine when I wasn't. Or how I resented having to go through the charade of pretending everything was as usual, when nothing was as usual. Nothing at all. One time—it was the closest

I ever dared get to it—I said, "Aren't you afraid?"

And Martin said, "No."

Was he afraid? I don't know. He must have been.

I was afraid. And I was aching to talk about it. Usually I am a very private woman, but during these months I talked to people at any and every opportunity. Strangers. People for whom I wouldn't have to role-play.

I traveled a lot on my job. And on trains and planes I created every possible occasion to tell strangers, absolute strangers, that my husband was dying. One time on the shuttle to Boston, my seat-mate asked, "Are you as nervous as you look? Are you afraid of flying?" He was very kind and concerned.

I found myself saying, "No, I'm not scared of flying. My husband has cancer. He's dying."

During those deathwatch months I had absolutely no interest in sex. No energy for it. No desire for it. At the same time, I was conscious of myself as a sexual being. To me, sex is an affirmation of life. And as Martin came closer to death, I hated the thought that men would no longer see me in sexual terms, but only as a widow. And I hated myself for this initial infidelity of thought. No man stirred my passions. Martin was my love. And yet I wanted men to see me as a woman.

On a business trip to Los Angeles, I chatted with the man beside me. He bought me several drinks and he dropped me off at my hotel. By coincidence, we met at the terminal (and there's a word that still makes me shiver every time I see it) two days later. We were on the same flight back to New York. Again we had a few drinks. We flirted and laughed. He offered me a lift into the city. I accepted. He suggested we stop at his apartment for a nightcap. I accepted that, too.

We were laughing. It was all unreal. It was a mad moment and I didn't want it to stop. He called me "Bellissima," and he kissed me. And then we were in his bed.

I remember thinking, "Oh, this isn't me, Lynn Caine. This is someone else." I stayed there very late. I had too much to drink. When I finally got home in the light of early morning, I looked at myself in the mirror—wild-eyed, haggard, hair a mess, a wreck. I'd been up for almost twenty-four hours.

"Is this what's going to become of you?" I asked that creature in the mirror. "You'll jump into bed with any man who gives you a drink and calls you 'Bellissima'?" I was scared to death in that hangover dawn. I felt vulnerable. And I was bitter because I had been so "available." It was a nightmare episode. Tawdry.

This period was filled with unreality. I made a lot of plans. Silly plans. I wrote to the Vermont Chamber of Commerce telling them that I was interested in buying a ski lodge. They put me in touch with a score of people. And I pursued this mad dream assiduously. I had suddenly decided that a ski lodge would be my salvation. Hard work, clean living, a good environment for the children.

This was the beginning of the craziness that seems to affect all widows. A ski lodge! A woman who keeps house the way I do? How could I manage to keep clean sheets on the beds? Or the bathrooms tidy? Or handle the drinks? Or buy the food? I *was* a good skier, but that was my only qualification. I think I had fantasies of meeting some wonderful laconic Vermonter who would appreciate and love and coddle a widow with two small children.

It was totally unrealistic of me to think I could manage a ski lodge. But I was serious. So serious that Jonny announced in school one day, "My mother's buying a ski lodge in Vermont."

Then I had a fantasy about Key West. I who prefer shadow to sun, who have never learned how to swim. I would move to Key West and somehow make a life and a living.

And I called an old friend in St. Louis and asked her and her husband to look into job openings for me there. I had convinced myself that St. Louis was the epitome of wholesome America and that wholesome America was what my children needed.

All through these crazy plans, I was pleased with myself. Pleased, verging on the smug. I preened myself on my practicality and foresight. I was dead serious. It was all part of a compulsion that I felt to move, move, faster, faster! Everything was changing. I had to change, too.

Common sense, or perhaps it was something in the stars, finally won out. I dropped the ski lodge, Key West and St. Louis early on. Martin never knew about any of my harebrained schemes and that is proof that deep down I knew that was exactly what they were.

The weeks went by. The time accelerated and yet it dragged. Martin was in and out of the hospital in Baltimore. I would marvel at the way this man with his pain, his weakness, his rotting body would manage to get himself into a taxi, into a train, into the hospital for treatment. The exercise of will was all.

Most of his remaining energies went into creating memories for the children. He was tortured by the knowledge that he would not see Jonny develop into a man, watch Buffy grow up to womanhood. And he desperately wanted them to remember him.

Martin took Jonny to Baltimore one week when he was an outpatient. They stayed at a motel close to the hospital. After Martin had his tests, he would come back to the motel and rest and then up he'd get and take Jonny to a museum, to a basketball game, sight-seeing. I don't know how he did it. What Jonny remembers best is the revolving dining room on top of the motel. That impressed him tremendously. They only ate there once because, as Jonny told me recently, "They served cuisine in the dining room, so Daddy took me to places where I could have a hamburger." How Martin would have loved his son's delicious choice of words. I wish, oh, how I wish that he could have heard it.

The other vivid memory Jonny has of that trip is that "Daddy vomited a lot." Poor Martin. He tried so hard. And he must have been so miserable.

Martin need not have worried. The memories had already been made. What Jonny remembers very clearly and can refer to unself-consciously are

the day-by-day happenings of life. When he is com-
plimented on his swimming, my sturdy eleven-year-
old now says, "My father taught me how to swim.
He was a very good swimmer."

And whenever he's in an automobile, he never
fails to bring up the time "my father was doing
eighty-five, maybe even ninety, and a policeman
stopped him." Or the time Martin went through a
yellow light at an intersection in Florida and
another policeman stopped him. "My father explained that the rules were different in New York,"
Jonny will relate, "and so the policeman didn't give
him a ticket."

And Jonny remembers the trips he and his
father took each summer. Trips to the dump.
Wherever we rented a summer house, there was
always the chore of hauling garbage to the town
dump. I was touched recently when we visited a
friend in the country and Jonny volunteered to help
with the dump detail. He supervised the packing
up of the stacks of newspapers, the gathering of
the bottles for the recycling bin and the disposal of
the plastic bags of garbage. "I'm a dump expert,"
he said. "My father taught me what to do."

Those were the memories that stuck. Little
things, perhaps, but so important. A father who
taught his son how to swim, who liked to drive fast,
who knew how to handle trouble, who took his share
of the responsibility of a house. These are good
memories for a boy. Lessons in manhood. Jon is
reticent about some of his memories. They must
hurt. But he will never forget his father.

Martin arranged to have pictures taken. He particularly wanted some of himself with Buffy. "Jon will remember me," he said. "But Buffy is so young. She may forget me." The possibility tormented him. A friend of ours, a professional photographer, took hundreds of pictures. I haven't had them developed yet. I'm not ready for those memories. Not strong enough.

But Buffy remembers her daddy. There was the time Martin took her to an ice cream stand for peanut butter and jelly ice cream. "We were alone," she boasts. "Just me."

Martin would be amused at some of the memories. At the table, if Jonny slurps or talks with his mouth full, Buffy will say, "Daddy used to say 'No slurping while eating. And there'll be no gurgling either.'" And she laughs. She mimics Martin's intonation perfectly. Her daddy is still very much with her and for that I'm grateful.

I felt very guilty about the children in the months Martin was dying. I was not supportive enough, not loving enough. The truth was that I was absent. I was totally absorbed in Martin. He was my life. I tried hard to be concerned about the children, but they came second. And I'm afraid they felt it.

I was a divided woman. If I could isolate the major problem among all the problems in my life at that time, it was probably being split so many ways. I had a tremendous amount of guilt and confusion about apportioning my time. Martin and I wanted as much time together as possible. This set up an enormous conflict in me about what to share with the children and what not to share.

When I went to Baltimore to see Martin in the hospital, I rarely stayed overnight, because I wanted to be home when the children wakened in the morning. As Martin spent more time in the hospital, I was torn more and more. What did I owe to Martin? To myself? To the children? And, becoming increasingly important, the big question: what did I owe to my job? My job was my lifeline, my anchor, my future and the future of my children. It was a schizoid time.

I was always full of guilt. Sometimes I would find myself laughing. I would have forgotten what was going on in my life for a moment. Then, "How can I laugh?" I would chastize myself. "Martin is dying!"

The months went by and our life had the quality of those nightmares where in the middle of terror, the dreamer reassures himself, "It's just a dream. Soon I'll waken. It isn't true." But our nightmare was true.

6

"My Joyful Self"

Martin was sleeping, if you could call it sleep. He had fought the pain as long as he could and finally given himself a morphine injection. It still horrified me to watch my husband shoot up. I had a tremendous revulsion against drugs. But I had a tremendous revulsion against pain, too. Especially against seeing someone I loved eaten up with pain.

Now he lay there, pale, emaciated. I knew he would drowse for a few hours. Free of pain? I hoped so, but he was so restless that I knew the beast was there, surging against the drug. These days Martin never had a conscious moment without pain.

At night I would wake and the bed would be weaving with pain. I could feel it as Martin searched quietly, almost furtively, so as not to waken me, for a comfortable position, a way to rest. He would twist. He would turn. It was like being on a raft on the sea. I never considered moving to a separate bed, however. It was important to me that I be there if Martin wanted to talk, if he wanted to stretch out his hand and touch me.

I learned to do Yoga breathing. That often helped when I got tense from the horror of pain in the night. I would lie there on my side of the bed and make myself breathe deeply from the pit of my stomach slowly, slowly. In, in, in. Then out and out and out. I would will my body to relax from my toes to my scalp and then back down again.

I stood in the doorway of the bedroom watching Martin as he slept. The up and down of his chest comforted me. I knew he was alive. Even though I often wished he were dead, wished he would hurry up and die. "How much more of this can I be expected to take?" I would rage to myself. "And the children? How about them?"

I shivered. I was scared. I wanted Martin alive, vibrant, vain, arrogant, witty, endearing. I wanted his quicksilver mind, his lean body. His protection. My identity.

I had been around and around and around with these thoughts—a hundred times a day, a thousand times a night. I was beginning to look like a survivor of Buchenwald, big staring eyes, tautly drawn skin. I was full of fear. What does a woman do? I didn't know.

I tried as best I could to play the role of supportive wife, soon-to-be widow, gallant in the shadow of death. Greer Garson would have done it better. But I was no Mrs. Miniver. Perhaps if Noel Coward could have written the script? I considered Vivien Leigh's Scarlett O'Hara. She gave the role some of the mean wit I liked to think I possessed.

But in the face of death? I used to go around saying that Barbra Streisand couldn't play me when they made the movie. People would lift an eyebrow. They felt uncomfortable. "Lynn is so impossible," I could almost hear them say it. But I was more than half serious. What they didn't know was that Martin was directing this macabre divertissement. It was an act. We evaded and pretended. We never talked about his death now. If I brought it up, he dismissed it. "Come on now, darling, let's get on with it," he would say. No, head up, lips stiff, shoulders squared. Don't let the world know your heart is breaking, your love is dying, your life is coming to an end. Everything must go on. But all that went on was pain.

I began to realize how much I depended on Martin for my identity. What would I do when he was gone? I felt that I had indeed built my house upon sand, not rock. And it was all slipping away from me. Life's grains were sifting through Martin's fingers no matter how desperately he fought to hold on.

And Martin was a fighter. "Fuck you, God!" I screamed it a hundred times a day. "Let him stop fighting! Let him die! Let me get on with life!" I was daring God and I knew it. I didn't know how I could live after Martin died. All I knew was that I had to. I had two small children.

In the back of my mind all the time was the magnificent Jacqueline Kennedy in her widow's weeds holding a child by either hand. That was the way I wanted to play it. Dignified. Worthy of praise. Deserving of sympathy. But proud. And tender. And cherishing my children.

But I didn't cherish my children. I hated them. I hated those kids. Hated them! They were too much. When Martin was gone, how would I take care of them? What would I do? Who would marry me? What would *become* of me? Okay, you smartass God up there, what *will* become of me? You don't have any answers, do You? And You're supposed to be so almighty!

I was standing there by the bedroom door. Just letting all this free-float through my head. I did this all the time, without realizing it. The whole thing—my anxieties, my terror, my anger, my worries—would shiver through my head just the way they had shivered through my head ten minutes earlier. It was eight months since Martin got his death sentence. And it was getting worse all the time.

It was like the sickest Muzak tape any sadist could have spliced together. Martin's-dying . . . I-hate-him . . . Martin's-dying . . . What-will-be-come-of-me??? . . . Martin's-dying . . . I-wish-he'd hurry-up . . . Goddam him . . . Die-damn-you-die-Martin . . . No-Martin-live . . . I-love-you . . . I'll-not-exist-without-you . . . I'm nobody-without-you . . . Martin-how-can-you-do-this-to-me??? . . . And-the-children?

There it went again. I couldn't stop, couldn't stop, couldn't stop. I headed for the telephone. When things got too bad and I couldn't turn off that eerie fantasy tape, I'd call someone. That always helped.

I'd say, "Judy, I feel rotten."

And Judy would say, "Sure, Lynn. I know you feel rotten. Who wouldn't? Tell you what. Bring the kids over and we'll go bicycling in the park."

I'd say, "Irma, I feel rotten."

And she would say, "Sure, Lynn. Hang on in there. I'm coming over for a drink."

Friends helped. Just being there, listening, breathing, talking. They helped me feel I was still in touch with the world out there where nobody was dying. Just here, in our house, there was death all the time. Death breathing in my ear every night.

This evening before I got to the telephone, Jonny called out from the bathroom. "Mama, are you there?"

"Sure, Jonny, I'm here."

I went into the bathroom. He was in the tub. Both my children took their own baths practically from the moment they could crawl over the rim of the tub. I'm not saying they got awfully clean. Sometimes they just redistributed the dirt. Jonny's fingernails were still grimy, but his face was shining and he had a crown of soap suds that made him look like one of Puck's band in *A Midsummer Night's Dream*.

"What is it? You need your back scrubbed?"

"No," he said. "I was thinking. Mama, what are we going to do if Daddy dies?

"I won't have a father," he said.

And I said, "Baby, we're going to do as we've been doing. We're going to live just as we've been living. And don't you worry. I'll take care of you.

"We're going to be very sad, Jonny," I told him. "And very lonely for a long time. But one day we are going to be happy again, because we are happy people."

I paused. Then I asked, "What will you do?"

He considered. Then Jonny said an incredible thing. "I'm a very active person," he said thoughtfully. "And if I start doing things," and here he used a funny word for a little boy, "if I start doing things," he said, "I'll be my joyful self again."

That's what he said, his "joyful" self.

I tried to smile and I said, "Yes. Yes, that's the way it will be."

Then I had to leave the bathroom. I could feel my face crumpling; the hot tears came up in my eyes. I closed the door and stood outside in the hall, my head against the door. Oh, yes. Oh, yes. Martin is going to die. But will we ever be our joyful selves again? I don't know. Oh God, Jonny, I hope you're right. I waited for the tears. But they didn't come. They had stopped as soon as they started.

Jonny started splashing in the tub again. I hoped he'd get that soap out of his hair. I looked into the bedroom. Martin was lying there. Still. I watched to be sure he was breathing. I hoped that pain had disappeared in his drugged sleep, was not following him, relentlessly allowing him no escape. There had to be some respite for him. Martin, dear Martin, I will welcome death for your sake.

But all of me wanted to shake him, to say, "Wake up, darling. Let me tell you what Jonny just said. He's such a great kid. I'm so proud of him. Aren't you?"

I couldn't do it. Who will steal sleep from a dying man?

Life leaves little by little, sometimes slower, sometimes faster. And Martin was leaving us. The fact that I couldn't share Jonny's insight with his father was like a tick of the clock. Tick. So much closer to death. Tick. If Martin weren't dying, I could easily have saved such a story to share with him at dinner that night. But death forces immediacy upon you. If you can't say it, share it, do it, right now—well, you may never be able to say it or share it or do it.

And I never did tell Martin what Jonny said. I had the time. But I didn't have the strength. It would have hurt Martin. We prided ourselves on being a "classy" couple, but our emotions weren't classy. We were scared of them. Scared to death.

7

His "Own Minute of Running Time"

The end of summer had been the end of hope. Not that we acknowledged it. We didn't talk about it. Death did not exist in our vocabulary. It was too obscene.

We had been a couple who "communicated," as the jargon of the day has it. Our idea of a wonderful evening was one spent together talking. Until after midnight. Just the two of us.

But now there was nothing to talk about. Not for us. Sometimes we would be reading together in bed at night. I would put down my book and my eyes would fill with tears. I would move over closer to Martin and he would put his arm around me.

"Lynn, it is what it is."

He said that so many times. And there was no answer.

Often he would go on, "I know you're going to be all right. I know I don't have to worry about you."

There was no answer to that except the one I

always gave. I'd say, "Of course, darling. You don't have to worry about me."

Or he would say, "You're going to get married again, darling. I want you to. I know you will. You'll have someone to take care of you. I know you're not going to do anything foolish. You're not going to take up with anyone terrible."

And what was the answer to that? I didn't know then what I know now. There is no one to take care of me. I *did* do foolish things. And I *did* take up with someone terrible for a little while. Martin was wrong.

We had our bed-pillow litanies that we repeated over and over. I'd say, "I wish I'd been a better wife." I couldn't begin to count the times I said that.

Martin would respond, "You've always been the girl for me. The only one I ever wanted to marry."

This helped, but the exchange that has helped me most came one afternoon. It must have been a Saturday. He was in bed and I permitted myself to beg, "Please, don't leave me."

And Martin said something that I have remembered every day of my life since then. He said, "Darling, when I'm gone, you're going to shake your fist at my photograph and shout, 'Why did you have to go and leave me, you bastard!'"

He was so right. The rage still keeps boiling up in me. But when I think of what he said about it, it makes me smile. And I don't feel quite so rotten mean when I'm angry.

There was a moment that last year when we

were particularly close, tenderly close. It was perhaps the last time we felt truly close, the two of
us. One evening shortly after we came back to
the city from Vermont, Martin said, "Let's go out
for a walk."

It was dusk. A particularly lovely time of
day. I was pleased that Martin felt strong enough
to walk. We crossed the street into Central Park
and paced slowly down to the pond. It was the
quick time between daylight and the dark. We sat
on a bench by the water and held hands. We didn't
say a word. And it was an inexpressibly sweet
hour.

Later I thought of all the times he had asked
me to go for a walk and I was too tired or too
busy or just didn't want to. Too lazy. Self-reproach
and guilt are so devastating—like a tarnish over
your emotions. I wish the memory of that twilight
hour were not shadowed by the accumulated guilts
of the past.

As Martin's cancer gnawed away at him, we
grew apart, imperceptibly but irrevocably apart. I
would detect occasional flickers of resentment from
Martin, resentment that I was up and about life
while he was dying. It was intangible, yet very real.
No matter how close you are, how loving you are,
there come moments when you suddenly understand that no matter how well you communicate,
you are not communicating at all.

I began to sense that Martin was in a totally
different dimension from the one I was living in.
I would ask myself, "What is he thinking? Does he
resent me? Does he hate me?"

And with blind trust I would assure myself, "Oh, no! No! Martin's not like that. He's too generous to resent, to hate." But of course he did.

There were times when I would feel this resentment almost physically. It wafted through the air like a cold draft, damply chilling like a current from an underground cave. It would go away, then come back.

There were other times when I would say to myself, "What the hell am I doing here? I'm talking about the future. And he has no future."

During the last months of Martin's life, I felt very strongly that I was being selfish. Extremely selfish. And this changed our relationship, too. I became self-conscious. I would find myself chattering away to him about something inconsequential, but interesting to me, that had happened at the office, and he would say nothing, simply look at me. He never said, "What the hell do I care? Here I am dying and you're going on and on about who said what to whom."

But I understood that his whole perception was different. He was removed from me, from us. And I hated him for it. At the same time I did understand. Lillian Hellman put it so beautifully when she wrote about having the same kind of alienated feelings toward Dashiell Hammett. "I was so often silent angry with Hammett," she wrote, "for making the situation hard for me, not knowing then that the dying do not, should not, be asked to think about anything but their own minute of running time."

And Martin and I knew that his own minute was running out.

Yet Martin tried. I knew he did. If ever I had doubts, they disappeared the last time I saw him. It was in the hospital in Baltimore, in that room I had come to know so well. Martin had told me on the telephone the night before, "Don't come down. Don't come." But I had to.

When I walked in, he was conscious. He asked, "What day is it?"

"Saturday," I told him.

"Do I have to be coherent for you now, darling?" he asked.

"No, baby," I said. "Go to sleep."

And he said, "Stay."

I stayed. He was full of morphine. He drifted off. I don't know where. He didn't know I was there. I sat there—sad and full of the most aching kind of love. How often I had underestimated Martin! Never given him credit for the tremendous effort he made to spare us all. Sometimes even hated him for it. The most magnificent gifts of love may be like that, accepted by the recipients as their due with no understanding, no conception of the effort, of the price in life's sweet energy. With that last question to me, Martin had confirmed his love. I know he would have struggled to stay conscious, to remain coherent for seconds, possibly minutes, if I had needed him, if I had asked him.

Yes, he was concerned with his "own minute of running time," but he never lost sight of us in our more generously paced dimension.

That day in Baltimore was a century long. Yet

it passed in a flash. I sat by Martin's bed. Doctors and nurses came and went. Suddenly it was dark. A young doctor came in and put his hand on my shoulder.

"Come on, Mrs. Caine," he said. "You know there's nothing you can do for him. He's drugged to oblivion. I don't know how long it will last.

"Go home to your children," the young doctor told me. "That's where you belong. With your children."

He was right. Martin didn't know I was there. The children needed me desperately. I went back to New York that night. And I never saw Martin again.

8

No More

Martin was in a coma. The doctors told me not to come to Baltimore. He would never come out of it, they said. But Martin was a fighter. He fought for life. Each day the doctors were amazed that he was still alive. Alive. Day after day after day. A week. Twelve days. Thirteen days.

I felt guilty. I should be there. No, the doctors said. You don't have to do a death vigil the way they do in the movies. Martin would not know. Would never know. Stay home with your children. I believed them. I knew there was nothing I could do for Martin. It would have been an exercise in masochism. But I still felt guilty.

I felt guilty. And I felt sick. I was walking around in a daze. One morning I called the office and told them I wasn't well, that I would not be in. I never did this. Chills, fever, diarrhea, hangover, cramps, no matter what, I always showed up in the morning. But not today. I could not get moving. I didn't know what was wrong with me, but I could barely drag myself to the bathroom. In the middle of the morning, the door opened and there was Jonny.

"What are you doing home?" I asked.

"I vomited in school, all over my project," he said, "and they sent me home."

He did look green. I told him to get into his pajamas and we were both sitting in my room feeling miserable when the telephone rang. "That must be the hospital," I said.

Jonny perked up and said to my amazement, "Maybe Daddy is cured."

I could hardly believe my ears. "No, son," I said. "Daddy can't be cured."

I reproached myself for his optimism. We had tried to be truthful with the children, but we had slid around the fact of death. I had comforted my-self that children pick up so much that is in the air that they did not need death spelled out for them. They knew. But obviously they didn't. We had per-mitted Jonny to hope when no hope was permissible.

As I got up to answer that ringing telephone, a whole scene flashed through my head. It had been months ago. Harold's wife, Vivian, had driven me and Jonny to the hospital. It had been arranged that Martin would come to the window and wave at his son. We had set this up because Jonny was so obvi-ously distressed, so unhappy without his father. And children are not allowed in hospitals, part of the inhuman bureaucracy of institutions.

So that morning Jonny and I and Vivian stood outside and from five floors up, Martin waved to his son. Jonny did nothing. He looked up at the window.

"There's Daddy," I said. "Wave to him."

Very tentatively, Jonny raised his arm. Finally he waved.

I went back into the hospital to say good-bye and Vivian walked to the car with Jonny.

"Wasn't it nice to see Daddy?" she asked.

"That wasn't my father," Jonny said firmly.

When she told me about this, I was very upset. I called Harold. "Isn't there some way you can get Jon into the hospital so he can get it through his head that it is his father in there and that he is very ill?"

Harold wasn't convinced that this was the right thing to do, but he agreed. The following week he arranged to have Martin brought down to the lobby in a wheelchair so Jonny could talk to him and get a hug and a kiss and know that it was his daddy.

I may have overreacted to all this, but I had had such a strong feeling all along that Martin's denial of approaching death, his refusal to talk about it, was wrong, that I could not permit Jonny to indulge in the same denial. He had to face the fact that his father was in the hospital, not off on a business trip or whatever fantasy he was spinning in his head. But I had not succeeded. Jonny still had hope.

But I was not in Baltimore. I was home and Jonny was with me. The telephone was still ringing. I had to shake myself back to reality.

It was the hospital. The young doctor who had told me to go home to my children two weeks earlier.

"Your husband died this morning," he told me.

I don't know what I said. What do you say to the man who tells you your husband is dead? Thank you? I have no idea.

Recently I asked Jonny, "Did I cry?"

"No," he said. "You were acting brave." Acting brave! Children are so aware of what is going on. He knew all about role-playing. Why hadn't he known about death?

So at last Martin died. No more pain. No more hope. No more denial. No more fighting for life.

No more.

It was the end.

9

The Great Memorial Cocktail Party

Now I had a new role. Widow. And I was going to play it magnificently. Make way, Jackie Kennedy.

Martin was dead. And I didn't know what had happened. I was numb. But I didn't know I was numb. I didn't even know I had been hurt.

I was the practical woman of affairs, rising to the occasion. I made the arrangements. All the arrangements. All by myself.

I called the mortician in Baltimore. Martin had told me at the very beginning that he wanted to be cremated. But what to do with the ashes? Months ago, I had had hilariously macabre discussions with the mortician about this problem. He hinted that it was possible to scatter the ashes surreptitiously over Arlington Cemetery, a service, he indicated, that he performed for many families. But, of course, in the special language of death, the mortician did not say "ashes"; he referred to them as the "cremains." I shuddered and I giggled every time he used the word. Just as he never said "your husband" but rather "your loved one," and "when he dies" always became "when he passes on." No wonder there is so little reality about death. Even the people who make a living from it can't accept it.

We finally arranged that the ashes would stay in Baltimore tucked away in some cubbyhole or other. I couldn't have cared less. What are ashes? But I had had to play the concerned, responsible, soon-to-be bereaved wife for the mortician. Now I called him, told him that Martin was waiting for him in the morgue.

I had no feeling about any of this. It had to be done. I did it. I didn't cry. I didn't choke up. It was like phoning in the grocery order. As I made all the necessary calls to family and friends, I prided myself on how cool I was, how controlled.

My friends were marvelous. A lot of them brought me food, and that's just about the most helpful thing anyone can do. One woman made a big jar of spaghetti sauce, grated a bowlful of cheese and mixed a fruit salad. She packed it in a basket and left it at the door with a note: "I know the kids like spaghetti. Try this for lunch." I was grateful, not only for the gesture, but for the fact that she didn't need to see my gratitude.

Other friends came by with casseroles, home-baked brownies, brandy. Neighbors asked the children over for lunch and supper. One blessed woman friend wrote a note saying, "Life must go on. I want you to know that alone as you are, you are not alone. If you need anything—laundry toting, babysitting, grocery shopping, company, money, anything at all at any hour of the night or day—I am here waiting to help."

All this was so kind, so good. Because indeed the children must be fed, the house must be cleaned, hair must be combed, baths must be taken, beds must be changed, telephones answered. Life does go on.

I started pulling together a memorial service for Martin. I called all the people I wanted to have around me. It was a very small group. The chapel only held fifty people. I was insistent that my friends bring their children. And they did.

Jonny and Buffy were very much involved in everything. And it was good for them to have all the bustling about. If it was comforting for me, it must have been doubly comforting for them, because they had been neglected so often during Martin's last months. Now we were together, the three of us. They were all I had. I was all they had.

Jonny wanted me to get dressed up for the memorial service. Liké his father, he liked to see women in pretty clothes. I had a beautiful flowered dressing gown with a ruffle around the neck that Martin had bought me a long time ago. Jonny loved it and urged me to wear it. It was a charming fancy. And his instincts were correct. The memorial service should not be morbid. I wanted to look my best for Martin and the world. I wore Martin's favorite dress, a pale blue wool. And Buffy wore her best "party dress," sprinkled with tiny flowers and smocked at the yoke. She looked adorable. One of my friends had to rush out and buy a jacket for Jonny because he didn't own one.

I don't remember much about the service. It was short. I recall thinking about the impression I was making as I walked down the aisle holding Jonny and Buffy by the hand.

I had asked Harold to deliver the eulogy. That's too formal a word. It was simply a man saying a few words in remembrance of a friend he had loved and respected. The prose was awkward, but sincere. It was very moving and I think that it comforted many people.

"Emotions did not come easily to Marty," Harold said. "He was a man of the mind; a man who believed in will and intellect; that all of life's problems are capable of logical and rational solution. Of powerful intelligence, rapid grasp, and prodigious memory, he was at times computer-like in response or recall.

"Marty was honest and courageous. He had the courage to be honest with himself—as well as any man can—to face what he saw and so to be honest with the world.

"Marty was a lover of music and an opera buff. He used to go about singing arias in a cracked, tuneless tenor which drew its ancestry from the chants of muezzins in their towers. His feigned indignation if one did not recognize the aria was a delight. Last summer, which he spent in Vermont soaking in the music, was I believe the happiest of his life.

"Marty was proud. He was proud of his wife, whom he adored. He was proud of his son, who pleased and gratified him. He was proud of his daughter, whose antics captivated and enchanted him.

"Had he no faults, he would not have been human. We need not discuss them; suffice it to say he was human.

"Now our friend is dead. He did not believe in a hereafter. Still he is with us in

> *"That best portion of a good man's life,*
> *His little, nameless, unremembered acts*
> *Of kindness and love."*

That was all. That was Martin.

Afterwards everyone came to the apartment. I had expected that we would sit there, subdued, talking about Martin, wiping away a few tears. Being tender, thoughtful, mourning him. But it was not like that at all. It was an enormous cocktail party. And I think it was the best thing that could have happened. I needed people around. I needed to talk. I wasn't ready to mourn. This was a terrible moment and I needed a bridge of people to help me cross it. Martin was dead. Martin was nothing but ashes now. My husband was dead.

Slowly a sense of the difference that now existed between me and the rest of the world was emerging. I was at a cocktail party, but I wasn't participating. I wasn't saying, "Try this. Have one of these. There are more in the kitchen." I wasn't asking one of the men to nip down to the liquor store and get some more bourbon.

I was there. Smiling. Talking. Telling the children to quiet down. They were all running through the house, having a terrific time. Everybody was having a great time. I emptied a few ashtrays.

And I kept asking myself, "What am I doing

here? Why am I talking? And laughing? What am I laughing at?" Then it dawned on me that I wasn't laughing. My guests were all having a good time and I was out of it. I was left out.

Suddenly I felt like death. It was only three days ago that Martin had died, that the telephone call from Baltimore had found me at home on a day when I felt too ill to go to work. My illness had disappeared with the phone call. I never gave it another thought. But now I was enormously tired and weak. There were still people there.

I can't remember anything after that, but one of my friends told me, "You said, 'I'm tired and I'm going to bed. Enjoy yourselves.' And then you disappeared."

It turned out that I had viral pneumonia and I was sick for three weeks.

And that was the end of that. Martin was finally dead. He was ashes. And when I eventually got up out of bed and went back to work, I knew I was a widow.

I went back to work before I should have. Terribly fatigued, a fatigue that was to haunt me for months and months. But I was afraid of losing my job. I have to point out here that my office was utterly sympathetic and understanding. Nothing had been said, done or intimated that I could have interpreted as a threat to my job security. No, this was just part and parcel of the financial insecurities—some real, some imagined—that bedeviled me. I went back to work. I was full of antibiotics and I was starting a rotten new life.

Lynn Caine, widow.

10

P.S. Don't Tell *Me* How Bad You Feel!

A widow. A widow is different. It takes time to realize just how different. There was a transition period when every morning I had to grapple with the fact of Martin's death all over again. Every morning it was new. A raw wound that took a long time to heal over.

But in those early days, I discovered a marvelously soothing balm, the condolence letter. I had never before understood its function. If I thought of it at all, it was simply a duty like a bread-and-butter letter. But to the widow, a letter gives comfort without demanding the intimacy that she cannot give or, at least, that I could not give. I was grateful for the thought, the comfort, the remembrance. I was also grateful that I did not have to react instantly to show my gratitude. Letters were a source of strength, of comfort. Not all the condolence letters I received were comforting or strengthening. Too many lacked sympathy, sincerity; they reflected the writer's horror of death. But the good ones—they were marvelous.

WIDOW

One young man who had admired Martin very much drove down to Baltimore from New York to visit him in the hospital. He was shattered by the ravages of the disease. After some awkward conversation, he started crying and then told Martin that he loved him a lot and would miss him. And Martin said a wonderful thing. He managed a smile and said, "Now, that wasn't so hard to say, was it?"

The man told me about this in his condolence letter, which I received just a few days after Martin's death. It was so like Martin. And I felt very close to the writer, because he understood how much it would mean to me.

Of all the condolence letters—and I received close to three hundred—this was the one I read and reread and still reread. It comforts me. It captured the quality of Martin's spirit. And when the children are a little older, I will read it to them.

According to the little Webster's on my desk, condolence means "expression of sympathy with another in sorrow." But most of the condolence letters I received were anything but. Instead, they were expressions of personal awkwardness and discomfort, addressing themselves to the writer's distress, not to my sorrow or to our shared loss.

"I don't know what to say . . ."

"I'm bound to be lousy at offering polite condolences . . ."

"Several times I started to write expressing sympathy, but I can't find the words . . ."

"What I should say just won't come . . ."

"I feel even worse now . . ."

"I feel so inadequate and helpless . . ."

"Not much one can say at a time like this . . ."

"I wish there were something I could say or do . . ."

"I don't feel so cool trying to give words of comfort . . ."

What ego trips! I! I! I! These letters offered no comfort. No, that's wrong. They did. The fact that they came, that they were written, of course that counts for something. It made me feel good to find a fat bunch of letters in the mail, but apart from that—nothing. So many letters, like those from which I've quoted above, were totally negative and expressed nothing but what each writer felt about his or her own inadequacy.

It seems thankless to look a condolence letter in the eye—and scorn it. But obviously very few people know how to write one. I would like to help.

The brand-new widow, raw from loss, is in no mood to be told how awkward her loss makes others feel. Such a response from those around her is society's first step in convincing the widow that she is now a second-class citizen, because she makes other people uncomfortable.

None of my friends who sat down to write these duty letters wanted to make me feel bad. But I don't think they wanted to comfort me either. I am convinced that their main impetus was to discharge this distasteful duty, get it over with. No one is comfortable in the face of death. In fact, it is this very discomfort, probably, that makes it so difficult for them to think of ways to help the one who suffered the greatest loss. They just want to get that letter written, stamped and in the mailbox so they can *stop* thinking about it. After all, if they thought, they might feel.

And yet a good condolence letter is so easy to write. I received offers of help ranging from baby-sitting to grocery shopping. Expressions of faith in me. Words of sympathy for the hurt and loneliness. There was nothing complicated about these letters, but the writers were so obviously identifying with me in my grief that it comforted me to know that others understood how I felt. Women, understandably, were the most perceptive and sympathetic. But many men wrote sensitive letters, too.

How does one write a good condolence letter? With tender loving care, as one treats so many of life's injuries, big and small.

Keep in mind that the widow is shaken. Alone. Insecure. So don't tell her how bad you feel. She can one-up you in spades. It is graceful to state that you understand how the bereaved is feeling, that you sympathize with her and that you are sorry she is so miserable. It infuriated me to have people say, "I know you'll be feeling better soon." I wanted people to sympathize with how terrible I felt right then and there. To acknowledge my raw distress.

Offer comfort. And comfort can be so many things. A remembrance like the little anecdote of how Martin said, "Now that wasn't so hard, was it?" An offer to take the children for a day or two. Or an invitation for a weekend to get away from everything.

But mean what you say. So many people wrote,

"You must come stay with us for a few days at the shore/in the country/at the lake." And I would have been very grateful for this respite. But no one extended a definite invitation, no one followed up with a date and a time. And this was hard. A widow feels so alone in the world, and then when friends seemingly let her down, it is just another blow making her feel even more alone.

Finally, think of the widow, not of yourself. So many letters were just additional turns of the screw, full of expressions of how uneasy the writers felt, how miserable the writers were—as if they expected *me* to comfort *them.* At that moment, I was so drained, I could barely comfort my children. These letters made emotional demands on me that I could not meet. I found them distressing, even enraging.

Letters need not be long. One comforting message from an old friend was simply, "Get well from everything quick." She was referring to the pneumonia that had sent me to bed on the evening of Martin's memorial service as well as to my bereavement. I felt that she understood how I was suffering in every part of me.

Letters need not even be terribly personal. Here is one from a stranger:

"I'm an attorney who has never had the pleasure of meeting you. I did, however, have the privilege of knowing and working with Martin. His intellect, courage and wit were his outstanding attributes as an attorney and as a man. I hope you will accept my deepest condolences."

Letters need not be serious. A little humor

makes life brighter for a moment. A colleague wrote:

"I was terribly saddened to hear about Martin's death and I want you to know that I've been thinking about you a lot. Let me know if you want a bank robbed or any other troublesome job done, like deporting difficult authors to Vietnam."

Praise is wonderfully welcome. The widow feels so vulnerable. This letter made me feel good:

"Your courage and philosophy of living affected all of us who had contact with you in this period and will, I am sure, enable you and your children to extract the fullest from the future."

Emotion and understanding are best of all. This letter, sweetly understanding and staunchly encouraging, helped me through several dark hours. It came from another widow.

"Heart's been with you, if no words. I know too much—and not enough—about living with death so close. I know what it is, but I do not know for you, because each of us has our own way to go. I know that you are brave and beautiful and that you were married to a man worth the loving. I know that we are luckier than most, but that is only minor comfort when your good man fades.

"Don't be angry. Believe that it is all worth what you must pay. Hope that you may understand why, but try not to demand that you do. Trust time. Continue loving."

This was a most generous letter. It gave of the writer. Of her heart, her emotions, her wisdom. And it helped me.

P.S. Don't Tell Me *How Bad You Feel!*

So when there is concern, let it show. If you love, well, as Martin pointed out, it's not really so hard to speak of your love. Just let your feelings come out.

Part Two

THE SEASONS OF GRIEF

11

As Spring Follows Winter

"I know of only one functional psychiatric disorder whose cause is known, whose features are distinctive and whose course is usually predictable. And that is grief, the reaction to loss," says Dr. Colin Murray Parkes, an eminent British psychiatrist and a member of the Tavistock Institute in London. And yet this "disorder," he complains, is not even touched on in "most of the best known general textbooks of psychiatry."

Unbelievable? Not really. I can understand why death and grief are so neglected, even by the professionals. Death is the last taboo in our society. We are terrified of it, much as the aborigines were terrified of an eclipse. And with far less reason. After all, dying is the ultimate human task. Although it is the end of life, it is part of life and we must learn to accept it. The deaths of others affect our lives up to the very moment of our own. Our lives can be richer if we accept death as a fact, not a taboo.

WIDOW

Since every death diminishes us a little, we grieve—not so much for the death as for ourselves. And the widow's grief is the sharpest of all, because she has lost the most. But few people understand that grief can represent emotional growth, an enrichment of the self. It is cruel that women are not educated in the progress of grief, since so many of us face the absolutely inevitable prospect of widowhood. Other cultures, other ages laid down protocols of behavior which, no matter how rigid they may seem to us, were at least a guideline for widows to grasp as they suffered through the various stages of grief. But today, widows have little to guide them. The various efforts to help bereaved women—widow-to-widow services, funeral home booklets, efforts of banks and brokerage houses looking for "widow's mite" accounts, even the courses in death now offered by some universities and colleges—are nothing but a Hansel and Gretel trail of bread crumbs. They are no guide to grief. Society's distaste for death is so great that widows tend to become invisible women. They are disturbing reminders of mortality and grief. Yet we are all mortal. And grief is a healing process, not a disease.

If only someone whom I respected had sat me down after Martin died and said, "Now, Lynn, bereavement is a wound. It's like being very, very badly hurt. But you are healthy. You are strong. You will recover. But recovery will be slow. You will grieve and that is painful. And your grief will have many stages, but all of them will be healing. Little by little, you will be whole again. And you will be a stronger person. Just as a broken bone knits and becomes stronger than before, so will you."

If that someone had said this, what would have happened? Knowing me, I suspect that I would have protested, "Oh, that's very interesting. I'm sure you're right. But it doesn't apply to me. My case is different. You see, I . . ." And I would have gone on to explain that mine was a very special case indeed.

But perhaps not. I like to think I would have had the sense to benefit from such wise counsel, that I would have asked, just as one asks the doctor when told that surgery is necessary, "What will it entail? How long will it take? How much will it hurt? When will I be my joyful self again?"

There are no pat answers to such sweeping questions. They vary with each individual according to temperament, background, emotional and physical health, age and a host of other conditions. But there is a pattern. Grief is predictable. Studies in this country and in England have corroborated that there are phases of grief and that phase follows phase as spring follows winter.

And each phase has its use. There is no avoiding the natural progression of grief—nor should one want to. In this country, devoted as we are to the pursuit of happiness, we tend to forget that happiness has its price and that love must be paid for. And the coin with which some of us pay is grief. Amazingly, in the course of paying, one discovers a synergistic effect. By experiencing one's grief and accepting it, one grows in warmth, in understanding and in wisdom. I can testify that while my grief has been a bitter burden, it has also changed me and made me more aware of the importance of living each "minute of running time" to the utmost.

I am convinced that if I had known the facts of grief before I had to experience them, it would not have made my grief less intense, not have lessened my misery, minimized my loss or quietened my anger. No, none of these things. But it would have allowed me hope. It would have given me courage. I would have known that once my grief was worked through, I would be joyful again. Not my old self. I am another woman now. And I like this woman better. But it was a hard birth. I hope that this chronicle of my grief may help other women, give them hope, add to their strength and eventually aid them in finding their own true identities.

12

When Feeling Stops

The first stage of grief is merciful—a numbness that comes with shock. In my case, it started before Martin died. I had become inured to many horrors. I had reached the point that when I walked through the children's cancer ward in Baltimore, the young victims, emaciated with sad, staring eyes, no longer moved me. I didn't cry when I learned of Martin's death. And I walked through the memorial service and the days that followed without a quiver, without crying.

"I felt numb and solid for a week," said one young widow whose husband had died unexpectedly. "It was a blessing . . . everything goes hard inside you like a heavy weight." She was sure that she could not have managed the children and the funeral arrangements without this numbness. She did not cry during this week either. But then her feelings came flooding back. Other women experience a much longer period of numbness.

A reporter who visited Mrs. Lyndon B. Johnson six months after the President's death wrote, "Lady Bird is as composed and gracious as she was in the White House, greeting callers with the same wide smile and vibrant enthusiasm that she displayed when Lyndon was alive." When the reporter marveled at this, Mrs. Johnson explained, "Grief carries its own anesthesia. It gets you over a lot."

And it does. I don't know how I could have functioned without that anesthesia. When the dying was over, the little ceremonial flurry subsided and friends withdrawn to carry on their own lives, I would have been lost without that blessed numbness.

I presented a brave front to the world. It was no longer role playing. I was truly the Little Spartan. But with a difference. I didn't feel the grief gnawing away at me. At a luncheon with some colleagues a few weeks after Martin died, I was getting off such brave lines as, "I'm going to be all right. I'll get married again. I know I will." They were impressed by my control, but the truth was that I didn't yet know what had hit me.

I used to wonder in a dazed way when it would begin to hurt. I found out soon enough. Feeling crept back nerve by nerve, and five months after Martin died I was a quivering wreck.

But until then I walked through my days like a robot. I went to work. Came home. Took the children to the park on weekends. Cleaned out Martin's closet and drawers.

Now I flinch and wonder how I ever did it. But I did. Took down his suits hanging in their orderly rows and gave them away. Packed up his shoes,

each one polished and toeing some invisible, Martin-
ordained line with its mate. Cleaned out his dresser
drawer with the cuff links and studs and all his
neatly arranged masculine paraphernalia. Gave almost everything away. I kept Martin's cuff links
and studs for Jonny. I kept one of his warm coats.
Don't ask me why.

And his old Viyella robe, a Black Watch plaid
that he had worn and worn. It smelled of Martin.
I started wearing it. It dragged around my ankles,
but I pulled the sash tight and felt comforted in it.
I'd come home from work and get into that old robe
every night. There came a time when I would put
it on Friday nights and droop around the house in
it all weekend. It was months before I realized that
I was getting very peculiar about that bathrobe—
and threw it away. It was heartbreaking. I felt
guilty. I knew it was simply a raggedy old robe,
but emotionally it was Martin still embracing me,
still comforting me. When I threw it out, I felt I
had committed a little murder and would be pun-
ished.

Little by little I began to feel. I fought against
it. I became very self-protective, spent a lot of time
in bed, clinging to my tattered cocoon. I craved
softness now, blandness. The refrigerator was filled
with vanilla ice cream and apricot yogurt. But there
was no escape. I began to feel. Began to hurt.

13

Crazy Lady

When that protective fog of numbness had finally dissipated, life became truly terrifying. I was full of grief, choked with unshed tears, overwhelmed by the responsibility of bringing up two children alone, panicked about my financial situation, almost immobilized by the stomach-wrenching, head-splitting pain of realizing that I was alone. My psychic pain was such that putting a load of dirty clothes in the washing machine, taking out the vacuum cleaner, making up a grocery list, all the utterly routine household chores, loomed like Herculean labors.

I was alone. Alone. Without Martin. Forever. And I didn't know what to do. I was beset with problems, some real, most imagined. I did not know how or where to start to put my life in order. If only I had known that the wisest course of action was inaction. Doing nothing at all. At least until I had regained the ability to cope with the essentials of everyday life.

If that hypothetical wise person had existed

who would have told me about grief's seasons, he would have also stressed that the widow has no conception of what she is doing for many, many months after her husband's death.

Helen Hayes, the actress, confessed, "For two years [after her husband's death] I was just as crazy as you can be and still be at large. I didn't have any really normal minutes during those two years. It wasn't just grief. It was total confusion. I was nutty," Miss Hayes said, "and that's the truth. How did I come out of it? I don't know, because I didn't know when I was in it that I was in it."

I didn't know I was in it either; all I knew was that I hurt. But looking back, I was certainly a crazy lady. Oh, I thought I was eminently sane, that I was making wise decisions. But I was acting like an idiot.

And I was idiotically inconsistent. I swung from outlandish attempts to solve my problems (and money loomed the largest; I equated it with security and stability) to maudlin, childish endeavors to set the clock back and try to pick up the threads of my life from the years before I knew Martin. Few of my actions had much to do with reality. They were freakish, inconsistent. Crazy.

That's really what it was. Craziness.

I was not prepared for craziness. But it was inevitable. Folk wisdom knows all about the crazy season. Friends and acquaintances tell the widow, "Sit tight. Do nothing. Make no changes. Coast for a few months. Wait . . . wait . . . wait." But the widow, while she hears the words, does not get the message. She believes that her actions are discreet, deliberate, careful, responsible.

I certainly did. I believed that every step I made was carefully thought out, wisely calculated. But the record shows otherwise.

One bizarre caper of mine was to write a rich politician.

"You are fat and rich; I am poor and thin," I wrote. "My husband died leaving me with no life insurance and two small children to support on a publishing salary. Would you please send me $500,000.

"I met you at a literary cocktail party in Washington last year and you drove me to the airport.

"I look forward to hearing from you."

Crazy! It was one of those things that one might have fantasies about, but never, never do. I did it. And I expected him to reply. Every night I'd riffle through the mail. I knew what the check would look like. It would be bright yellow and the amount would be typewritten. $500,000.

Finally it came. An envelope in the mail. A typewritten letter on the politician's official letterhead.

"Sorry, I cannot comply with your request," he wrote.

I was crushed. Heartbroken. What had I expected? I'm afraid I had expected a check for half a million dollars.

This was just the tip of the iceberg. My craziness went deep. I was a lost child and yearned for someone to take care of me, to love me. Anyone.

Before I met Martin, I had had a love affair

that ended disastrously. Very unpleasant and messy. Yet, less than two months after Martin died, I telephoned that man. For some reason, I thought he would still be waiting for me. As I dialed the number, that same old number of eighteen years ago, I had a fantasy that he would send me yellow roses and promise to cherish me forever.

When he answered I said, "You told me I could always call you if I were in trouble." I started crying. "I'm in very bad trouble," I sobbed. "Martin is dead and I have two children."

He didn't know who I was!

"It's Lynn," I told him. "'You said you'd never be able to forget my eyes." I stammered through half a dozen reminiscences, determined that he must remember me. It was terribly embarrassing. When I finally had the sense to hang up, I sat huddled in the chair by the telephone for the rest of the evening.

Most of my craziness involved money and security. I was terrified because Martin had left no insurance and the money had stopped. This was realistic enough. A widow with two children has to be concerned with money. What was unrealistic was that I never stopped to consider the fact that I was still earning a decent salary and that I was now getting Social Security payments for the children. We were certainly not going to starve. But somehow, after Martin died I was possessed with the idea that I was penniless.

Today it is a shock to realize my financial incompetence at the time. It ranged from the trivial to the staggering. When Martin was alive, I used his credit card to telephone home every night when I was out of town on business. One evening after he died, I started dialing home from Boston. And I panicked. "Martin's dead!" It hit me hard, as if for the first time. "I can't use his credit card any more. And I don't have enough change to make the call." There I was in a public telephone booth at the airport, shaking and crying. It did not dawn on me that I could reverse the charges—although I had made collect calls all my life. And it took months before I realized I could apply for my own credit card.

There were other aberrations, less grotesque. I knew Martin was dead, but somehow it took a long time for the reality to seep in, become part of me. I would go to the supermarket and think, "Oh, they have endive today. I'd better get some. Martin likes it so much." I would pick out an avocado for him, a fruit I've never really liked. Then I would realize, "My God! He is dead!" and put the avocado back as if it were burning me.

When something funny happened, I'd say to myself, "Oh, wait until I tell Martin about this tonight! He'll never believe it." There were times in my office when I would stretch out my hand to the telephone to call him, to chat. Reality always intervened before I dialed that disconnected number.

I have learned that most widows do similar things. One woman told me it took weeks for her to stop setting the table for two every night. And another said that she had renewed her late husband's subscription to a motor car magazine for three years running although she hadn't the slightest interest in automobiles herself and never took the magazines out of their wrappers. She simply stacked them beside his easy chair month after month until it dawned on her that this was crazy.

One day when I was on the Fifth Avenue bus I spotted a man who looked like Martin. I pulled the cord and plunged after him. I knew it wasn't Martin, but I tried desperately to catch up with him. I couldn't. I lost sight of him and it made me very depressed, as if Martin had rejected me.

And I had dreams. I would dream that I heard the door open while I was in the kitchen getting the ice for our evening drink. It was Martin, home from work. I would be so happy to hear him come in. But I always woke up before I saw him.

I had a sense of Martin, of some quality of Martin that had filtered into me. A very real feeling that part of me was Martin.

I thought this was some very special psychic phenomenon until I discovered that it was not peculiar to me at all, but part of the phenomenon of grief. Dr. Parkes reported that one widow who participated in a study of bereavement insisted, "My husband is in me, right through and through. I can feel him in me doing everything."

My identification was not this strong. But I very often felt like some character in a Victorian novel, the young widow, for instance, whose husband has died and left her alone to run the family estate. She lies in bed at night mulling over some problem that she must cope with the next day. "What would the squire tell me to do?" she wonders. And in her sleep, the answer is given. When she wakes in the morning, her thoughts are clear, she knows how to proceed. For many months, I would routinely think to myself, "What would Martin tell me to do?" when faced with some problem. I usually came up with a satisfactory answer. I still do it, but much less often. I have learned that the best answers come from myself. I no longer have to rely on the dreary mystique of "Martin knows best."

There is nothing shameful about the widow's temporary insanity. It is remarkable, in fact, that so many widows are able to live through this distressingly crazy time and come out as strong or stronger than they were before.

A psychiatrist, Dr. Thomas Holmes, has isolated forty-three events or crises that the average person may expect to experience and given them stress ratings, which he calls "life change units." The death of a spouse, by far the most stressful, is rated at one hundred life change units. Change in one's financial status, something experienced by most widows, has a rating of thirty-eight. And if the change involves the widow having to go to work, there are an additional twenty-six life change units to add on.

I had not known about stress ratings before I was widowed. If I had, it might have helped me proceed with a bit more caution. As it was I accumulated more life change units in the course of a year than I could handle. According to Dr. Holmes's rating, this is how mine added up:

Death of spouse	100
Change in financial state	38
Mortgage over $10,000	31
Change in living conditions	25
Revision of personal habits	24
Change in residence	20
Change in social activities	18
Change in sleeping habits	16
Change in eating habits	15
Christmas	12

A psyche-shattering total of 299 life change units. Dr. Holmes's research showed that an accumulation of 200 or more life change units in a year is usually more than a person can cope with. He advises people with 200 or more units to "lie low" for a little while and suggests that it is a good idea to talk things over with a physician or a qualified counselor.*

If anyone had intimated that I was not supremely sane and suggested that I could use some counseling, I would have been insulted. Unbelieving. I would have retorted, "If ever I have been practical in my life, if ever I have measured my words and actions, this has been the time." I was convinced that everything I was doing made sense. The truth was that most of it was nonsense. It took

---

* Here are stress ratings for other life crises that widows may encounter:

Death of close family member (other than spouse)	63
Personal injury or illness	53
Change to different line of work	36
Foreclosure of mortgage or loan	30
Son or daughter leaving home	29
Trouble with in-laws	29
Change in work hours or conditions	20
Vacation	13

me a long time to undo some of the ridiculous—and expensive—mistakes I made. And the emotional fallout verged on the disastrous. I did eventually reach the point where I sought counseling. But if I had understood earlier the unbearable degree of stress I was subjecting myself to . . . Well, what then? I like to think that it might have stopped me from acting so precipitously, thus reducing the number of life change units I accumulated. And I like to think I would not have played the Little Spartan so long and would have gotten the psychological help I needed earlier.

14

So Good for the Children

Most of my ridiculous actions—asking a politician I had met once in my life for half a million dollars, trying to revive a love affair that was eighteen years dead—these were all minor crazinesses. They pale in the face of other insanities I committed. The major one was moving.

Within three months after Martin died, I had given up our comfortable apartment in Manhattan, bought a house I hated across the river in Hackensack, New Jersey, pulled the children out of their New York schools and enrolled them in new suburban schools, embraced a way of life that did not appeal to me, that I was not suited for, could not afford and could not cope with. I was absolutely irresponsible and crazy. And even today I can't explain exactly what was going through my head.

Part of it, certainly, had to do with the fact that I clutched at anyone and everyone after Martin died. But most of all I clutched at Harold and Vivian. For more than fifteen years the four of us had shared Thanksgivings. Gone to the opera together. Rejoiced over our children together. Spent weekends together. And in the last year, Martin's dying had united us in a tight bond of misery.

Now I looked upon Harold as a surrogate Martin, a heavy burden to place on a busy doctor with his own wife and children. When he and Vivian suggested I move to Hackensack to be near them, I let myself be persuaded. I wanted to be. I wanted someone to make decisions for me. At that time if someone had said with sufficient authority, "You've got to see the Dalai Lama," I would have taken the next plane for Nepal or Tibet or whatever. Anything that involved action.

I had to do something. That, of course, is the trap most widows fall into. The most difficult advice in the world to follow is "Do nothing."

On one level, my brain was functioning. It was telling me not to move. The suburbs were alien to me. I have always been a city woman. I like crowds and bustle and stimulation. I like apartment living, where if anything goes wrong you call the super. I am spectacularly incompetent. When I put a plug in the wall, a fuse blows. And I did not know how to drive. What would I do in the suburbs?

Harold and Vivian reassured me. I would be in the city every day, they reminded me. Working. Their handyman would be glad to take care of any repairs I might have. Besides that, he would shovel my snow and mow my lawn. As for not being able to drive, a few lessons would remedy that.

On another level, I was in the grip of the most compelling financial insanity, although at the time

I considered that I was being eminently prudent and foresighted. My mind was going $200 for mortgage payments in Hackensack versus $450 for rent in New York. It was going $4,000 for private school fees versus nothing for public schools in Hackensack. I never stopped to think that Buffy and Jon could go to public schools in Manhattan as well as in Hackensack. And I never once considered that furnaces need oil, houses must be painted, washing machines break down, toilets get clogged or any of the other expensive facts of suburban existence. I never counted the cost of commuting. Enormous. I never considered the cost of moving. Eight hundred dollars each way. I never counted the cost in time—less time to spend with the children, less time to see friends, less time to shop (supermarkets in Hackensack weren't open when I got home from work the way they were in the city). It took months and months for me to come to my financial senses.

And there were the children.

A colleague took me out for a drink after work one evening and asked, "What in hell are you moving to New Jersey for?"

"It will be so good for the children," I said.

He shook his head. "Lynn, you're crazy. Don't do anything unless it is good for you. Your children have to live their lives. They will grow up. They will leave you. And where are you going to be?" he concluded dramatically.

"In New Jersey," I answered softly.

And so the decision was made.

If I had only understood the dynamics of bereavement! Widows fight against the realization of their loss. They know their husbands are dead, but still there is a part of the mind that resists, that won't accept. My frenzy of activity, my moving, my refusal to listen to the friends who said "Take it easy"—all this, I am convinced, was a frantic postponing of the moment when I would have to face widowhood. Perhaps if I had understood the forces at work, I could have accepted that wise advice everyone gave me: "Don't make a move." But how is a widow to know that she is not in control? The answer, I have learned, is that you don't have to know. Just take it on faith. You are *not* in control. No matter what you think.

And so I moved. Into a pretty little suburban box with green in front and a stone wall in the back. It had a picture window, the bus stop was around the corner and there was a basement where the children could play on rainy days. I hated it. As soon as the moving van left, I knew I had made a terrible mistake.

What was I doing in Hackensack, New Jersey? After the first forty-eight hours, I used to think to myself, "Martin is dead. But I've gone to hell. It's not fair!"

There was one bright spot. The teen-age son of Harold and Vivian. He helped a great deal—with the children, running errands, driving me around (I never did get a driver's license). Once I asked him what he would have thought about my household if he had been a man from Mars and was reporting his observations.

"What would a man from Mars say? Well, he

would probably start off with 'Wow! What a scruffy lawn!

" 'Different from the other lawns. Full of junk. Papers. Kids' toys. The garbage can out front all week long, not just on Wednesdays. The grass higher than the other lawns. And no metal machine in the garage!

" 'The children are like the other children on the block. They ride bicycles and play ball and jump rope and run around. But the mother! The mother does not belong to a church or a club. She does not go to PTA. She does not talk to her neighbors. When you ask the children where she is, they say, "She's asleep." ' "

He was right. My house was different. It was a mess. So was the yard. And there was no car in the garage, because I could not learn to drive. Every morning for weeks, I got up at six-thirty and took a driving lesson. Every morning I got a little worse. The driving instructor finally suggested I stop wasting my money. And I agreed happily.

But without a car, not knowing how to drive, I was as truly stranded in this suburb as if I were on a raft at sea. I was absolutely dependent on my friends. And I resented that passionately.

Helen Hayes said that she flinched when she looked back at her crazy period. "I was most unattractive," she said. "Unreliable and erratic. I squabbled . . . I had never done that before. I took umbrage at nothing at all."

She could have been describing me.

When it became clear to me that Harold and Vivian had their own lives, that they could not be the surrogates for Martin that I had childishly cast them as, I felt let down and angry. Our friendship could not withstand the stress. The cords that bound us snapped and soon we were polite strangers. If the three of us had understood the psychology of grief, perhaps the friendship would have survived. I don't know.

It is not uncommon for widows to break with old and dear friends. The root cause of the break is the widow's search for someone to fill her husband's place in her heart, in her life. And friends cannot be expected to do that.

"The loss of a husband may or may not mean the loss of a sexual partner, companion, accountant, gardener, babysitter, audience, bed warmer and so on," explains Dr. Parkes, the English psychiatrist. "Now the widow [searches for] surrogates who can perform similar services." She also is trying to learn how to fill some of those roles herself. This task has to be accomplished without the help of the one person in the world who the widow has been accustomed to rely on, her husband. When she has children who are also grieving and needing comfort, this places "a major burden on a woman over and above the fact of the bereavement itself."

Without this friendship, I was very much alone. If it had not been for my mother, I could not have coped. She had agreed to come live with us and I was so grateful. I needed her. All your life when you are sick or in trouble, all you want is your mother. And mine gave of herself without stint. Both to me and to her grandchildren. Without her, the children would have suffered even more than they did.

I had really believed that the move would be good for the children. And it was in some ways. They had a certain physical freedom they didn't have in the city. But they were isolated, too. From me. The one important fact that I did not take into consideration was that nothing could be good for the children if it was not good for me. Our emotional and physical well-being is so closely interlocked that I must be healthy and functioning (and that adds up to happy) if I am to be able to give them the love and time and support they deserve and need. And they did not get it. They were not getting enough love in that year I spent in the hell that Hackensack represented for me, because I did not have enough to give. I tried. Yes, I did. But I failed. I was too crazy, too sad, too lonely.

15

Four O'Clock
in the Morning

If there is a hell, it cannot be any more searing than the state I was in the year and a half after Martin's death. I progressed from numbness to craziness to panic. A mad acceleration of misery. At first, I thought that if only I could cry, the tears would provide a lubricant to ease the scraping terrors. I wanted to cry. I wanted to cry so much that it hurt. But I couldn't.

I started to be conscious of two enormous lumps inside me. They were growing. I could feel them. One in my throat and one behind my eyes, where I was convinced my unshed tears were accumulating.

Jonny was distressed that I didn't cry. "Gaga [that's what the children call my mother] misses Daddy more than you do," he reproached me one day.

"Why do you say that?"

"Because Gaga cried when Daddy died. Sometimes she cries now. And you never cry." He was defiant.

"I know," I told him. "I can't cry. But it's not because I don't miss Daddy. It's because I miss him so much."

That didn't make any sense to him. I could tell that. But it was the truth. And what else can you tell a child?

I got rid of the lump in my throat. One evening I was working late. Feeling terrible. Sorry for myself. Angry at the world. Wounded. Bewildered. I didn't know what to do. Another woman was still there. I asked her to come with me. "I have to scream," I explained idiotically. It was after six and the building was practically empty. I called the elevator. Pushed the button for the top floor. And I started screaming. Long wailing screams. No words. Like an animal. I pushed the hold button and kept on screaming. It seemed like hours, but it was more like a minute. I felt an enormous relief, the kind of exhausted peace one has after vomiting. And the lump in my throat was gone. My throat was sore and raw. I felt as if I had had surgery. My companion put her arm around me and said, "I'm going to take you home now."

I still have that lump of dammed-up tears. I don't know really why I can't cry for Martin. I can cry over a book, at the sad parts in movies, at weddings. But not for Martin. It took me a year to be able to cry for my father. How long will it take for Martin?

I started having cancer dreams. I would dream that Jonny had cancer. Or Buffy. Or I would have it and the children would be orphans. I dreamed a lot about the children in the cancer ward in Baltimore. And I had a recurring dream about taking Jonny and Buffy to the doctor. It was always the same.

The doctor would examine the children and then call me into his office to talk. His face would be grave and I would know what he was going to say. "Mrs. Caine," said my dream doctor, "both Jonathan and Elizabeth have cancer and they are going to die."

I would say, "You've made a mistake. God did it once. He can't do it again."

"No, Mrs. Caine. Make no mistake. They are going to die."

I would awaken, grinding my teeth and hearing the word "die . . . die . . . die" in some nightmare echo chamber. My heart would be beating so fast I would be weak. The palms of my hands would be wet. And the nightly grinding of my teeth resulted in a condition called bruxism which eventually necessitated expensive dental work. I wouldn't be able to go back to sleep. And I would walk through the next day in a cloud of fatigue.

The loss of sleep made me tense and irritable and I would take it out on the children and my mother when I got home at night. This distressed me enormously. Tranquilizers would help, I decided. Harold gave me a prescription for a small number, but made it clear that he would prefer I not take them.

"It's better to feel your grief," he said, "you'll get over it faster that way." But I didn't believe him. He was right, of course, but I couldn't accept that any more than I could accept any of the good advice people were giving me. I asked my dentist for a prescription. And then I started "borrowing" tranquilizers from my friends. I was a mess and getting worse. I began waking up at four o'clock every morning with those terrible cancer nightmares.

Later I learned that they were just one more phase of grief—the stage of protest, denial and disbelief. Some women have mild hallucinations that they have seen their husband, something like the time I saw a man who looked so much like Martin that I jumped off the bus and started running after him. Some women have actual hallucinations. One woman was absolutely convinced that she had seen her late husband sitting at his desk going through his papers one evening when she walked past his study door. When she rushed back to see him, he had disappeared.

Many women have these denial dreams. Most of them deal with the husband still being alive, but the dream can take many forms. Mine were always that I or the children had cancer. This was a way of identifying with Martin. This kind of identification, psychiatrists say, is like saying that the dead person is still alive. I was experiencing Martin's cancer symptoms. A way of saying that he was in me. My way of keeping him alive, of denying his death, because I was still unable to believe it.

There is even an explanation for the eerie way my nightmares woke me at four every morning. People have distinctive sleep patterns, as individual as fingerprints. And their dreams come almost on schedule, like phantom freight trains full of emotions. My sleep pattern was such that four o'clock in the morning was my vulnerable time, when I would awake in shuddering terror.

This would have been a sensible time for me to get some help, professional help from a therapist who knew about bereavement and loss. But I didn't have the sense. "This can't last forever," I told myself. I was quite right. It got worse.

Panic struck. I started having acute anxiety attacks. I think the world divides itself into two kinds of people: those who know the feeling of such an attack and those who don't.

I have never been so afraid in my life. I would be sitting at my desk and I would start shaking. My heart would race. My skin would be clammy. I thought I would break up. Or was it break down? Or I would be on the street, on my way from here to there, and suddenly—an anxiety attack. I'd be huddling in a doorway. Scared to death. Cowering. The worst ones came at night. I'd wake locked in a fetal ball. Every muscle tense. Afraid to breathe.

A friend who belonged to Alcoholics Anonymous persuaded me to try their techniques. They would help, she said. And they did. They had wonderfully effective coping mechanisms. The first thing I learned was "Move the body."

It sounds so simple, but it works. Now when panic struck in the night, I would tell myself, "Move the body." It took tremendous effort, but I forced myself out of bed and onto the floor to do exercises. "You only have to do ten." I would tell myself, "but do them. Move the body. One and two and three and . . ." It helped a lot. Then I bought a stationary exercise bicycle. That was even better.

When I woke up trembling in a cold sweat, I'd say, "If I can only get on that bicycle and do it twenty-five times." I learned not to set great demands on myself but to do things by the "nibble method." And I could just barely manage the nibbles. I would get myself out of bed. That was almost the hardest part. Get over to the bicycle and pedal twenty-five revolutions. That got the blood going. And immediately I felt a little better. Just to be doing something, anything, is better than cowering in bed. Sometimes I would grab that handlebar and pedal and pedal until I was exhausted.

Another coping mechanism—once I had got the blood flowing and was more in control of myself—was to go downstairs and make coffee, heavily laced with honey for quick energy. There I would be, at four in the morning, padding around a cold kitchen in Hackensack of all places, making coffee. I couldn't believe it.

All these coping mechanisms helped. But I wasn't getting enough sleep. When I got home from work, I fled to my bed. It was my solace. My comfort. I couldn't wait to get into it. I coveted sleep. I had no time, no energy for the children. All I could think of was getting enough rest so I could get up the next morning and limp through another dreadful day.

16

Dear Paper Psychiatrist . . .

Between cancer nightmares and anxiety attacks, my nights were horrors. I'd collapse into bed around nine and wake up at three or four. Tense, shivering, frightened. Alone. Blessedly, I stumbled on another coping mechanism. I started writing. I kept a stack of ruled yellow legal pads by my bed and when I woke up, I'd start writing. It helped.

I called the yellow pad my Paper Psychiatrist. I accumulated hundreds and hundreds of pages. Most of them I threw away. I didn't want the children to discover them. They were vile. Full of bad language, self-pity, despair. Here are some excerpts from the early months in Hackensack.

* * * *

It's 3:30. I have so much to do. Must learn to drive. Must get it together. Went to bed at midnight. Too late for me now. Need eight, not six hours. Must try to get a cleaning woman. Must keep slogging along. Must have my little washing-dressing-breakfast hour with Buffy this morning. Perhaps I can avoid the serious psychological problems she is bound to have. Love, love, love. That's what Buffy needs. I'm beginning to doubt that I have any any-more.

*   *   *   *

Did you know I start my driving lessons Saturday? That is if I pass the written test on Wednesday. Now that I have the school, the driving, the commuting together, all I have to worry about is the house, Social Security, the Veterans Administration, the bank and the big one—the taxes. I had no idea of how well off I used to be. I hope I'll be well off again. That's a fantasy. I know it. But it's better to be optimistic. I'm not as young and beautiful as I used to be and I'm not helping by neglecting my looks. No exercise for a long time. No hairdresser. Having some money would help. My face is beginning to line and I haven't been using night cream. Must do that right now. Oh, what an effective list this is. On to taxes and face cream. It's 4:30 and I may even catch a little sleep.

*   *   *   *

Jonny did not do himself proud today. Was self-conscious and up-tight. He really tried too hard and came on fresh. Smart-ass. His telling people I was crazy wasn't pleasant. Buffy is really a charmer. So is Jon. I hope he'll calm down soon. He's a fine boy, as Martin used to say. Why couldn't he have lived longer. I miss him so much and the children miss having a father so much. What a bum-rap-un-lucky-break-misfortune-fucking-cheat! I can't bear it. What drivel. What self-pity. How undignified I'm becoming. I've become everything I hate most.

How dependent I've made myself. My pain is so intense and has been for so long. Must get my hair done. I can't go on with this. Please read for a while. Surrender to that sleeping pill. I have very few sleeping pills left. I wish my order from S. would come through. Then there's V. But I have no access to him now. Harold won't give me a thing. When my sources run dry, I'll really be in a mess. I'm still big in the Compazine department with two more refills. And thus junkies are made. Anything to keep going.

*   *   *   *

I'm not dealing with things too well. I'm haunted by money worries extended to job worries exacerbated by inability-to-function worries. I don't really believe I have to worry about my job. I must call the gas company. There's gas escaping. One way out. Now let's explore feelings with money. Dare I hope I'll get something from the VA? Wouldn't that be fabulous? Won't it be a relief when the tax situation is resolved? If only I were a skillful writer, I could supplement my income. My fantasies are running away with me. But maybe this slogging away in the middle of the night will help. Practice, practice, practice. Even this drivel and drivel it is. Should I ever feel confident and energetic enough to do any writing, I certainly have something to write about—

A Hack from Hackensack

The Willies of Widowhood

How to Feel Sorry for Yourself Without Even
   Trying

Ten Ways to Destroy Yourself (including ac-

quiring an old stove complete with a faulty
pilot light which causes gas to leak)

How to Become a Junkie Like a Lady

Make no mistake. There are endless topics. It's
simply a matter of choosing one and settling down
to write.

* * * *

That full-length mirror I'm afraid to buy is a neces-
sity. Perhaps if I buy it, I'll look better, forced to
confront the mess I've let myself become. Vanity,
vanity. The surest way to insanity. I must stop being
self-indulgent. Must lose weight. Must exercise.
Must brush my hair. Burgeoning, blooming, wallow-
ing in misery. The only thing that's blossoming is
my skin and I have the occasional acne pustule to
prove it. Yuck, acne pustules, joyfully spared in
adolescence, hard to accept in senescence. Oh, joy.
More reasons for misery. How happy I should be!
Living with my mother in the suburbs. Insufficient
money. Two little children for whom I'm solely responsible. Learning how to drive with a mental
block as big as the Ritz. No energy. Nightmares
nightly. No social life. The worst has happened.
The future looks hopeless. Why am I punishing
myself so much? On the other hand, why make anything easy? Why spare myself any torture? Why
allow myself any relief? Such acute misery is rarely
attainable, so make the most of it.

* * * *

Obviously I have nothing to write about. I can't
inspire other indigent widows by my courage and
capabilities, by my true-to-life experience. Making
myself helpless and knowing it every step of the

way is nothing to write about. There's that marvelous Lynn Caine, clearly a survivor. Moved to the suburbs. Changed her life. Here's that supergallant, courageous little widow. Taking dope. Resenting her children, mother and friends. Letting her face and figure go to pot. Smoking up a storm. Goofing off. Adorable! And don't forget fucking up Social Security, Veterans Administration and taxes. Yum, yum that gas smells good. Asphyxiation self-taught. Go light the pilot, you jerk. You're in trouble. Maybe some help would be helpful. But first try the pilot. You can't afford a therapist. Everything depends on my lighting the pilot. I did it. I did it. I did it. Simply read the instructions on the stove. No more gas leaking. Is everything I've been avoiding this simple?

* * * *

Poor little up-tight Jonny. Returned home late from work to find Jon and Mother in a flap. Jonny guilty as sin, poor baby, for bugging Mother. Later when he worried about his hair and clean clothes for school, I was unsympathetic and yelled at him at the very time he needed relief and reassurance. All in all it was a horrible evening. Mother handled it incredibly well. Worst of all, I was unsympathetic when Jonny needed me and I feel terrible about it. I realize why I've been in a suicidal depression for the past few days. With no calendar on the wall, I had no curse reminder, no good old skull and crossbones. There it was, good old premenstrual tension. With my period has come enormous relief. It's good to feel human again. At least, semihuman.

* * * *

I made a great effort to get over to school yesterday and Lucy [a young woman who lived on our block] who was to drive us home arrived late. "I'll get you into a car pool when you learn how to drive," she blurted out. "My husband and I are separating and we're putting the house on the market. My psychologist says I need a new start, a complete change." "God," I said to the Higher Power, "what are You doing to me?" Well, good-bye Lucy. Buffy will miss your kids. And I'll miss the relief of knowing the kids' transportation problem was solved. Lucy, how could you do this to me, a poor, driven, disconsolate, terrified, lonely widow? Why couldn't you have a good marriage so you wouldn't have to break up your home so that my kids would have yours for companionship and a ride to school every morning? Lucy, how could you do this to me after all I've been through?

* * * *

I have no social life here at all. What have I done? Cut myself off from everything and everyone I love. Oh, Martin, my dearest darling, you sure screwed me. Left me unprotected. And my despair at your negligence is hurting me something fierce. Well, it is day now so I'd best get on with it.

* * * *

Arrived at office to find myself deluged with calls. So many calls, both incoming and outgoing, that I broke lunch date. When I got home Vivian took me to the market. She was annoyed with me, which in turn got me annoyed at her. This dependence is hard to live with. It's not my nature. But I can't learn how to drive, so no food can be obtained, no step taken without her and I resent it with all my heart. So, no doubt, does she. I can't go back to sleep, because I'm washing Jon's clothes and I have to wait to kick the machine when it gets stuck on "Spin." I'd like two more hours of sleep. I need them. Lorraine says, "There's a master plan. It's hard to understand, but everything is for a reason." The only master plan I can map out is that God had a plan to transplant me to the place of my destiny, Hackensack. Or maybe he got rid of Martin first and has me on his list to get next because His master plan involves the children. Perhaps He's planning to orphan them as part of their destiny. First though, He's planning to keep me on the rack and I ain't seen nothing yet. Things could get worse. I must be very strong about the day-to-day aches and itches. Unfortunately, my breaking point is close. There must be a solution, but I'm damned if I can think of it. I've really trapped myself by buying this house, but there was no other way. When I read these jottings, I realize how chaotic my thoughts are. Disconnected. Disoriented. Muddled. Messy. Dirty. Will I ever like myself again? Will I ever find serenity? Tomorrow, see Lynn Caine put through the wringer. Will she cope? See the next installment of "On the Rack" tomorrow at 4 A.M., brought to you by God, The Fuck of Master Plan, Inc., those wonderful folks who gave you "Strike Martin Down with Cancer."

* * * *

A good night's sleep for a change. Seven solid hours without awakening. No matter that it took two

Valiums. Things are looking slightly better and any little bit of better is great. It's the Valium, I'm sure. Apparently it blocks off that terrible anxiety. One reasonably smooth day is enough to make me tick well, but just one wrong note is enough to pitch me into the depths. How's my master plan, Goddear? What have You got coming up? Maybe a little breather? Let me work things out calmly for a change, maybe? Or do You have something really great in store? Like my daydream. A good man, maybe with a few kids and a lot of money, whose wife just died and he needs a lady to take over and fill his life with sunshine. He doesn't have to have all that much money, God. I take that part back. But enough so I don't have to worry. You're still on my side, aren't You? I'm counting on You, you know. And I know You won't let the children go down the drain, will You?

* * * *

Awoke with the horrors again. I know what to do now. Get up. Move the body. It will pass. Don't cower in bed curled up in the fetal position. Get up and smoke a cigarette. Oh, God, I promised Martin I would stop. He only asked me to do two things. Have a Pap test and stop smoking. I'll take the test. Wait for the horrors to pass. Cherish the children. They are loves. Take care of your looks. I must find the good people in this dreadful place. God, that driving rain doesn't help my paranoia. The world has gotten to be such a frightening place, so work, write, love the children. Be grateful for what's good. Don't succumb to self-pity. It is a killer. You're learning to grow up. And it hurts. What shit! Hang in. Work it through. Buffy. Whenever you resent her because life would be easier without her, kiss her, look at her, talk to her. She's so lovely, so responsible. SLIP. I meant *responsive*. I love her and I've got to keep straight about her. I owe her everything. She's such a tender little thing. She owes me nothing. How I wish the rain would let up. It's depressing as the backyard of hell. That's where I am.

* * * *

Squeaking through. Just. Felt good tonight. Coped well with little Buffy, who was so up-tight this morning. Day at work was dumb. Back home to Buff, who needs her time, no matter how short, alone with me. She was waiting for me, ready to be rejected, but I fooled her. We had a nice walk, a good chat, bought ice cream.

* * * *

Jimjam time again. It's boring and depressing here. I need some friends. Mother said, "You'll never get anyone as nice as Martin." True. No argument. But right now, I'm enraged at him. I'm told that is natural. Dying, leaving me to cope alone with two little children. Well, that's natural. But it's all those other things. His compulsive cleanliness about home and person, contrasted with the compulsive messiness, failure to consider the future. Messy in his head I mean. No money. No insurance. Poor me. Shit. Self-pity.

* * * *

And so it went. Dreary outpourings morning

after predawn morning. But they helped. If nothing else, writing it all down got me almighty bored with myself and my self-pity. I've always had a low tolerance for boredom. But I still had the horrors, the shakes, the panic attacks—and never, never enough sleep. On top of that there were the pills. I was walking around in a tranquilizer fog. Finally, one morning after I'd had my usual Lincoln Tunnel fantasy of being flushed down some vast white urinal as the commuter bus headed under the Hudson River for Manhattan, I realized I had to get out of Hackensack. No more Little Spartan.

As soon as I got into my office, I started calling friends and real estate agents about getting an apartment. I was moving back to the city, to where I felt at home.

I moved to Hackensack in August. Put the house up for sale in March. And the following August I moved back to New York. It was all very fast and crazy. After I had moved back, I said to one of my dearest friends, "How could you let me do such a goddamn stupid thing?"

He looked at me and said, "Well, I guess it was inevitable. Don't you remember when we talked about it?"

"No," I had to admit. "I don't."

"When I told you not to move," he said, "you looked at me very coldly and said, 'Don't be destructive.' There was no way to help you."

17

"You'll Shake Your Fist at Me"

There is another stage of grief. And that is anger. I remember the first time I came into contact with the anger of grief. It had been many years ago. Edward, an old friend of ours, had lost his wife. Another cancer death. (One learns that cancer is responsible for one out of four deaths.) Edward had adored Adele, and when she died he was shattered. Yet six months later, when he spent a summer weekend with Martin and me, I was shocked at his bitterness when he spoke of her. Savage criticisms came to the surface. That happy marriage—had it all been facade?

It was much later, when I was poring over books on child psychology after Jonny was born, that I discovered how very natural an accompaniment anger is of grief. It is the same kind of separation anxiety that a child feels toward the mother who "abandons" him (or so he feels) in the hospital when he is ill, or who "abandons" him when she leaves home to give birth to another child, or "abandons" him with his grandmother so she can go away for a weekend. Many mothers have had the experience of leaving a toddler for a day or two and returning to find him aloof and unloving. He is angry at her for leaving him.

When I read about separation anxiety I remembered Edward's reaction so long ago. Now I was experiencing it myself. And I was truly possessed by rage, just as Martin had warned me when he said, "You're going to shake your first at my photograph."

One researcher who observed twenty-two young and middle-aged widows discovered that eighteen of them experienced "excessive" anger during their first year of widowhood. One woman was angry at her late husband for not telling his doctor about his headaches earlier. Several were angry at the nurses and physicians who had cared for their husbands. Others became infuriated at friends and relatives. Some were angry at God.

A friend of mine took out her anger on her mother-in-law. Her husband, only thirty-two, had died a year before Martin. And there was one thing more than any other that fed Cynthia's rage. It could qualify for the sickest mother-in-law joke of all. But it was no joke. It was true. When Cynthia's husband had told his mother that he had leukemia, the distraught woman had shrieked, "How can you do this to me?" Unfortunate, but not really meaningful. Terror often robs us of our humanity—temporarily. However, Cynthia needed something to justify her anger. And she clutched at this stupid exclamation. "It's not the kind of thing you can talk about," Cynthia confided. "But every time I think of it, that ridiculous remark just floods me with bilious rage."

Other researchers have found that the younger the husband is when he dies, the angrier the wife. She feels that she has been cheated because he was not allowed to live out his allotted life span. "God didn't play fair," one widow said bitterly.

My anger shot out in all directions. At old friends. At my family. At my Hackensack neighbors. Even at my children. There were moments when I hated Jonny and Buffy. Times when I felt they were albatrosses around my neck.

It wasn't only the children. I hated myself, too. But most of all I hated Martin.

At the beginning I was full of compassion. But then as the dying went on and on, fury crept in. I was helpless. I couldn't save Martin. Couldn't keep him alive. Could not even spare him pain. Helplessness was too much to bear, so I became angry. And after he died, my anger took possession of me.

There were moments when I would switch from tenderness to rage in the space of a breath. I would think back to the day when Martin had told me, "It's going to be harder on you than on me," and, with tenderness, I would muse about how objective and considerate he had been. But then I would suddenly be more concerned with how hard it was on me. "It's easy to be objective," I would snarl, "when you don't have to face the music yourself." And my hatred and anger would flare up like an evil smoking mass that had just been waiting to ignite. That was the hardest rage of all to quench.

WIDOW

Years ago Martin taught me a technique for coping with pain. At one point I had had a great deal of pain and one evening when the doctor was not available immediately, Martin went into the bathroom and came out with a towel.

"Here," he said, "rip it as hard as you can, into a hundred pieces." I felt foolish, but as I tore that towel in half and then into strips I became completely caught up in the ripping. As if I were ripping out the pain that was tormenting me. One fury-ridden night, I discovered that the towel helped dissipate rage, too. So when that most evil of angers came upon me, I would go into the closet where I stored old linen, grab for a towel that had seen its best days and rip away.

My exercise bicycle was even better. If I could force myself to mount that bike and grip those handlebars and pedal away, my anger would eventually dissolve in sweat. I don't know how many hundreds of times my rage drove me to that bicycle or how many hundreds of stationary miles I pedaled working off my anger.

And, yes, there were times when I *did* shake my fist at his photograph—and then started laughing.

18

Breaking the Silence

Through all the months of nightmares and anxiety attacks, the woman I presented to the world was calm, coping, cool. Part of it was pride. But more of it was fear. I felt very insecure in a world that could allow Martin to die. What did fate have in store for *me*? I feared the worst. I had a dread of letting people sense my vulnerability. Like an animal, I feared that if anyone were to smell blood, it would be all over with me. No one should suspect how tormented I was, how worried, how very shaky. For if that became apparent, I was lost. I carefully concealed my terrors. Close friends, I know now, were concerned about me. They sensed my strain, my confusion. But my refusal to talk inhibited them from probing, from helping.

It was all part of the pattern that had been woven during Martin's illness. We had had tremendous difficulties in talking to the children about cancer and death. After our first attempt to explain it to Buffy and Jonny, we had found it close to impossible to discuss it further with them. We had an equal inability to talk to each other about our feelings.

But at that time I had been able to talk to others—to friends, to strangers. Especially to strangers. I had been able to spill out all my worries and fears about Martin's illness and inevitable death. But now the bad dream had come true. Now I was alone. And I could not talk.

"The widow is the center of a drama," explains sociologist Helena Lopata. "She needs to talk, to work it out." But I couldn't. I dared not talk about my feelings. Was this how Martin had felt? Had he been as frightened then as I was now? Was this why he had refused to talk about his feelings during all those months of dying?

One of the chores of grief involves going over and over in one's mind the circumstances that led to the death, the details of the death itself. Endless dwelling on the dead person. Memories are taken out and sifted. Finally the widow accepts the fact that her husband is dead. This is the reality. And talking about it helps make it real.

But just as I feared that I would be swept away by tears, that there would be nothing left, I was also too frightened to talk. I thought this was my own particular cowardice. But I discovered that it was the common condition.

Judith Viorst, the writer and a supremely articulate woman, also found that she could not talk about her feelings when confronted by death. "Three springs ago," she wrote in a magazine article, "my mother was dying—it took her several months—and she and I were together for hours each day. I sat beside her and held her hand; we spoke a lot of nonsense. But never, not once, did we mention why I was there. I sat beside her all those days. And yet she died without me. In love and in grief we couldn't talk about death.

"Maybe we all should begin to talk about death," she suggests. "The silence I've met on this subject shows we've been more frightened than we know, deprives us of each others' consolation and takes from us the gift of comforting too. . . . So let us talk about death."

She is right. We should. Talking helps. It helps the dying—and the living.

If Martin had been able to talk more easily, it would have helped him. Helped me. I suspect that we might not have engaged in so much role playing, but instead have talked to each other and to our friends about how we really felt—particularly about how Martin felt.

And, yes, it would have made our friends uncomfortable. But would that have been so bad? Today I think not. All of us face death. To talk about it, think about it, learn about it is to take some of the fear away, to weaken the taboo surrounding it.

I recently attended a memorial service for an old friend, a historian. The professor who eulogized his former colleague and friend described his handshake. It had been a gesture of utter sincerity, of friendship, of warmth. I remembered that every time I met the historian he shook my hand and I felt truly welcomed into his company. If only he had known before he died how much that hand-shake meant to everyone who knew him.

How comforting it would be to the dying to hear, while they still can, all the good things that their friends admire about them. Why should these things be left unsaid until after death?

We should talk. And we should learn to listen.

A friend of mine was very shaken when a colleague committed suicide. She had said "Good morning" and "Good night" to him five days a week for eight years. They had exchanged banalities about their work, their families, the weather. She didn't really like him, but when she learned that he had killed himself she was overwhelmed with grief and guilt. Guilt because she had not liked him. Had that contributed to his suicide? Guilt because she had never suspected the depth of his misery, never even understood that he was full of misery. Grief because he was dead. And, in dying, had taken a part of her life with him.

My friend talked to her husband about her feelings, but he was unsympathetic. "You're being morbid," he told her. "Stop dwelling on it. You're not going to do yourself any good by going over and over it," he said impatiently.

But he was wrong.

If she could have talked about it, my friend would have been able to come to terms with that death more easily. She had a real need to talk about the suicide and her feelings about the man. And her husband? Obviously, death scared him so much that he could not permit his wife to talk about it.

He could not listen. He was not able to help her with her grief work.

Sociologist Robert Fulton raised this problem in a conference on widowhood. "Whom can you turn to when you are touched by death?" he asked. His discomforting answer was, "There aren't very many people who are prepared to come to your assistance either socially or emotionally. In fact, it is sometimes hard to find anyone who will even talk to you about your loss."

Friends of Jacqueline Kennedy were shocked when, almost immediately after the President's assassination, she compulsively asked people, "Do you want to hear about it?" and rattled off each frame of that terrible sequence in her soft, shaken voice. But their shock reflected their ignorance. Mrs. Kennedy was instinctively helping herself to face the reality. Verbal repetition eventually dulls the horrendous shock enough so that it can be faced, can be accepted.

Talking helps us absorb less tragic situations, but even then, listeners tend to resist. People scoff at the woman who says, "Let me tell you about my operation." Why? Because it makes them feel uncomfortable. Vulnerable. Such intimations of mortality are frightening to most of us. Our fear outweighs our desire to help.

So from within and without, there are pressures on the widow not to talk. It takes strength to disregard them. Some women have such emotional sturdiness that they immediately set about the work of defining their loss and repeating its circumstances until the cruel edge is blunted enough for them to handle its reality. Other women require months before they can bring themselves to talk about their husbands, about their deaths. And until they can talk, they have not really started on the road to recovery.

There came a day when I knew that if I didn't have someone to talk to, I could not go on. But who? Who was there? Not only could I not talk about my grief, I had no one to talk about it to.

Family? I couldn't. The nuclear family is too small for talking. Our intimate world is so concentrated that when a member dies, our world contracts—sometimes to just one person. Other women have told me that they did not feel close enough or live close enough to the family members outside the nuclear group for those relatives to provide the support and comfort of the extended family of yesteryear.

Friends? Who wants to burden friends with sorrow? Who dares? The most truly helpful service a friend can perform is to listen patiently and sympathetically while the widow works through the various stages of grief. Too often, this is the one thing friends cannot do. It is too much for them. Too painful. They have not been educated to the widow's need to talk.

Friends want to help. To *do* something. Not only because the widow needs it, but because it makes them feel good about themselves. It feeds the ego. But it is the rare friend who understands the widow's need for a sympathetic listener. Rejoice if you have such a friend. But don't be disappointed if you don't.

Other widows? There are widow-to-widow organizations, a relatively new development, formed
to give recent widows the benefit of the experience
of other widows. Dr. Phyllis R. Silverman, director
of a program under the auspices of the Harvard
University Medical School, says that most of the
women who have benefited from the program em-
phasize the importance of being able to talk about
their feelings. "The volunteer widows are comfortable talking to the new widow about her grief," she
says. "They are able to listen, to be empathic and
to understand the turmoil of grief."

But independent women, inhibited women,
women who prize their privacy may resent this kind
of help and regard it as an intrusion. The time was
to come when I found tremendous comfort in talking to a widow whom I greatly admired. But she
was an old friend. I don't believe I would ever have
been able to confide my distress to a stranger who
came ringing my doorbell stretching out the hand of
widowhood, no matter how warm, how sympathetic
she might have been. And in some instances I think
this kind of interaction can be dangerous. It is
perilously easy for a volunteer widow to be tempted
to make a career of widowhood, to find her identity
as "widow." And the newly bereaved woman, frantically clutching at any stability, may also be drawn
into "professional" widowhood. But this is just my
own reaction. The only guide I can offer is that if
you think it would be helpful to talk with another
widow, then probably it will be.

Religious leaders? I belong to no organized
religion. But for those women who are truly re-

ligious, yes, their ministers, priests and rabbis may offer sympathy and good counsel and a patient ear. But then again, they may not. Too few have had training or experience in the needs of grief; too many offer the standard sympathetic clichés and fidget when confronted by the raw emotions of the bereaved. In one study of widows, the researchers were startled when woman after woman reported that the least helpful person had been her religious leader. So, by all means, seek consolation and support in religion. But if it is not to be found there, do not blame yourself as being lacking or unworthy. And do not lose hope.

For there is another source.

The widow should be aware that there are people to talk to, people who are qualified to listen, to help, to advise. For a fee. These are the psychologists and psychiatrists and all the other members of the helping professions. In our society, with its small, autonomous, isolated family units, they are invaluable.

Idealists may bristle at this as cynicism. But it is fact. The people one might have turned to naturally—priests and ministers, other widows, friends, family—cannot or do not want to cope with the wild, angry, desperate, sad, bewildered, tempestuous, endless talk of the grieving widow. Can all these traditional counselors and comforters be lacking the sympathy needed to listen? No, it is not exactly that. It has more to do with the way death has become invisible in our society. We have less experience with the dying (80 percent of us die alone in narrow hospital beds in strange sterile rooms), and the flailing emotions of the grieving make us too uncomfortable to listen.

Fortunately, we can turn to the helping professions. And they are aptly named. I would recommend that a widow who, like myself, finds she has difficulty in expressing her feelings and is suffering from this inability to talk, search out a trained therapist. Psychologist, psychiatrist, mental health worker—there are many choices and fees can range from moderate to high. However, women who live in cities with community mental health centers can usually arrange for professional help at minimal cost. The emphasis is on *trained*. Knowledge and objectivity as well as warmth are needed. Professionals will not inject their own unresolved hostilities or anxieties into your life as untrained friends, religious leaders, volunteer widows may do without meaning to.

I want to point out that a woman does not have to be in the state of absolute psychic distress that I had let myself reach in order to benefit from professional help. Nor do I want to push women who are working through their grief quite capably to feel that they need professional help. But if you are a widow who feels alone, who cannot talk about your feelings, who suffers from anxiety attacks and nightmares, who has problems with your children, don't try to be noble. Go get yourself some help.

How do you find a good therapist? It may take time if you don't live in a good-sized city. Ask your family doctor. Check with your local hospital, the county medical society, the local mental health association. Specify that you are looking for someone who has had experience in helping people cope with death. This will—or should—ensure that you don't end up with a therapist who has not come to terms with his or her own feelings about death and bereavement. Friends may suggest a psychologist or other counselor. Be sure to check their recommendations through the professional organizations mentioned above. After all, it is your own mental health that is at stake.

My therapist, a woman, was a source of strength from the first visit. She gave me a feeling of security. Suddenly I felt safe enough to talk. I no longer had to spill out my distress to an unresponsive pad of lined paper. The psychologist listened. And slowly, patiently, she guided me out of the maze of anxieties I had lost myself in. Together we examined my fears. As I talked about them, many disappeared. Others, I began to realize, were manageable. It was a great liberation.

I wish I had known about the therapeutic value of talk when Martin was dying. Because today I would insist on talking. I would talk to him about death and terror and pain as well as love. It is what you don't see, don't talk about, that terrifies you. The things that go bump in the emotional night. Talking dispels the phantoms. In helping Martin, I would have helped myself. I would have learned to talk about my feelings. And after Martin died, I could have talked about him. And talked about him and talked about him. Until I finally knew that he was dead and I was alone—starting a new life. I would have emerged from grief sooner. And so would the children.

Part Three

THE OTHER SIDE OF GRIEF

19

The Lonely Goose

"From the moment a goose realizes that the partner is missing, it loses all courage and flees even from the youngest and weakest geese. As its condition quickly becomes known to all the members of the colony, the lonely goose rapidly sinks to the lowest step in the ranking order. The goose can become extremely shy, reluctant to approach human beings and to come to the feeding place; the bird also develops a tendency to panic. . . ."

When I read this description of how the greylag goose responds to the loss of its mate in Konrad Lorenz's remarkable book *On Aggression* (Harcourt, Brace & World), I was unpleasantly startled. I didn't want to have that much in common with a goose. One sentence struck me on a particularly raw nerve: "The lonely goose rapidly sinks to the lowest step in the ranking order." That is exactly where I was. I had become a second-class citizen, a member of the invisible minority of widows. And like all members of minority groups, I was deprived—sexually, emotionally, socially and financially. My very identity was shaky. At times I felt practically nonexistent.

A male psychiatrist, full of puzzlement, wrote that the "loss of self reported by many widows" was mystifying to him. He quoted one widow as saying, "I feel as if half of myself is missing." Another woman told him of the "great emptiness" she felt.

"What do these statements mean?" the psychiatrist asked. "How can a person be full or empty?"

Only a man could ask these questions. A woman knows the answers. A widow feels empty and incomplete because, like most women, she gained her identity through marriage. And when her husband died, there she was. A widow. Empty. Without her husband to validate her existence. Without an identity of her own. Like geese, widows sink to the lowest step of the "ranking order."

Being a widow is like living in a country where nobody speaks your language. A country that considers you an untouchable. The ten million widows of the United States, despite their numbers, "share the characteristics of other minority groups that are targets of discrimination," says sociologist Helena Lopata. "They are women in a male-dominated society . . . without mates in a social network of couples."

One woman who was a source of comfort to me had been through a particularly tumultuous widowhood a decade before. I was very touched by her kindness and one day I remarked, "It must be hard for you. This must reopen all your old wounds."

She smiled. "Oh, no, dear. We are a sisterhood. Only women who have been through this can understand."

She was right. And one needs that understanding. Needs it desperately. But it can become addictive. This sisterhood can be dangerously seductive. It needn't be, but a widow must recognize the possibility—in order to avoid it.

I became aware of this through the experience of another widow, a psychiatrist who had always felt that she was very much in touch with her feelings because of her professional training. Nevertheless, when her husband died, she went through the same stages of grief with its denial and anger and craziness that other widows do. And discovered that seductive underground of widows.

"I found a whole new community of women," she told me. "Like an underground current. All the women who are alone. Swirling below the surface. I was never aware of them before. And now, even though I know I should be getting out into the world, that I should build a new life for myself beyond my work, I find that I am relaxing into this community—comfortable, comforted, content."

Her report on sinking into the world of lonely women was like an emotional trigger. It set off a jangle of alarm systems. All kinds of energy came pouring back into me. Like the extra charge of energy that danger unleashes.

A memory flashed through my head. A scene at an airport. I was waiting for my flight to be announced. A woman sat down beside me. Small, well-dressed, somehow birdlike. "Good morning," she said, "I'm Mrs. Wendell Willkie." Even then I was horrified. Her husband had died years before. But he was still providing her identity!

It was a chilling flashback. I thought to myself, "I'm not Mrs. Martin Caine. I'm Lynn Caine. Goddammit. I'm no wounded bird. No goose!"

20

Like a Penis in the Bank

I was ready to emerge on the other side of grief. I wanted to taste life again. To live, to work, to love. Suddenly I was frantically impatient with my whole way of life.

I retreated into my grief, but only briefly. More and more I wanted to clear away the worries and problems. There were days when I felt more whole, more capable than I ever had in my whole life.

It didn't last, of course. I wavered back and forth for months. But every day, I was stronger, more confident, more involved. Every day was a big step into a new phase of my life. Some of the steps were tentative. Sometimes I stumbled. But I moved.

One of the first things I had to set to rights was money. Money matters. It really does. It is right up there with love and security and identity. After Martin died, I used to wake up with my teeth clenched thinking, "You son of a bitch! You really screwed me! You selfish son of a bitch! You didn't love us enough to provide for our future. And now we're all alone. No husband. No father, No money."

Money! How could I be so bound up in money, crazily absorbed by money, fixated on money? Martin was dead. That was all that mattered. But I felt the loss of money almost as much as the loss of Martin. What mercenary devil had taken charge of my soul? No devil at all. I have come to recognize that money is important. Women should know more about it.

Freud is supposed to have said that money is like having a penis in the bank.* If so, he knew what he was talking about. Money is power.

---

* Widows, I have learned, tend to worry about money even when they don't have to. One woman, who had been married to a very successful doctor, said that when he died she had enormous financial anxieties—the wake-you-up-in-the-middle-of-the-night kind. So bad she could not concentrate on anything. Finally, her lawyer called her into his office. He said, "I was a good friend of your husband's and I want to talk to you seriously as a friend, not as a lawyer. But I want you to understand that I'm serious."

She was very puzzled. What was on his mind?

"I've watched you for the past three months," he said. "You have turned into a money maniac. All you do is worry about money. You have plenty. All you need. Your husband was very provident. He loved you very much. You have more money than you need.

"Now, I hope you believe me."

"Yes," my friend nodded. "Yes, I believe you."

"Then, for God's sake," and his voice turned harsh, "stop worrying about money. Start worrying about yourself. What are you going to do? You are in your early fifties. You have a good thirty to forty years ahead of you. What are you going to do with them? Turn your mind to that. You have enough money to do just about anything you want. As your husband's friend, I want you to start building your life. Stop worrying about money."

After she told me this, I told her what Freud had said about money being a penis in the bank. She laughed. "You know, I think that's exactly what it was. Money was my substitute for my husband. But it wasn't quite enough. That's why I was so worried and wanted more."

Strength. Life. It is sexual. I care more about money than I do about sex right now.

When Martin died, I lost so much—lover, confidant, companion, counselor—he was a thousand things to me. And at the same time, the money stopped. That last spending spree was over. It was time to pay the piper. But I had no money. And it was the one thing that could have taken Martin's place to some extent.

Money can't compensate two children for the loss of a father. Money can't reach out in the night and caress you. Money can't come home at night with a briefcase, a twinkle and a hug. But money can give you ease. And peace of mind.

And I had no peace of mind. Martin had left no insurance.

Martin's war, the one he had considered so romantic, had left him with his Silver Star, a tantalum plate in his head and a rating of 90 percent disability. This last entitled him to payments of about $300 a month for life.

We had always been financially comfortable. Martin made a good living. I worked—although publishing salaries are notoriously meager ("After all, you meet such interesting people"). And then there were those disability checks coming in every month. But because of that plate in his head, Martin had never been able to get commercial life insurance. He had applied three times, but each time, after his army record was checked, he had been turned down.

He did not even have GI insurance. In a quirky arrogance, Martin had disdained the ten-thousand-dollar GI insurance policy. "It's just peanuts," he scoffed. He was so wrong. It wasn't peanuts. It was peanut butter—and milk and hamburger and juice and shoes. It was the orthodontist and the pediatrician. It was summer camp.

The result was that when Martin died, there was just enough money for me to make the down payment on that house in Hackensack. The disability pension stopped instantly. If his death had been service-connected, the money—or at least some of it—would have continued. But, as the man at the Veterans Administration told me, "Cancer has an unknown etiology." What he meant was that unless I could prove that Martin's cancer was caused by his war wounds, I didn't have a case.

As a veteran's wife with minor children, I do get forty-three dollars for Jon and sixteen dollars for Buffy. I suppose I should be grateful for that. But I'm not. It just is not fair.

"I could die happy," Martin told me once, "if only I knew that you and the children were provided for." But we weren't. Despite his fourteen months of dying, he left our affairs in a terrible mess. Strange for a man who was scrupulously orderly. But he had never found the strength to straighten out our finances, to discuss how the children and I would manage on our soon-to-be rigorously reduced income. The strength to act, to initiate, to plan had left him.

But there had been no excuse for *my* inertia. I was not dying. I was a mother. I had children. And now I had those bitter sour-mouthed mornings when I cursed Martin. I wanted to hate him, but I couldn't. My conscience stood in the way. I had to ask myself, "Well, Lynn, what the hell did *you* do about it?" And that was a chiller. I had done nothing. This knowledge was part of that storm of anger that I launched at the world. So much of it was anger at myself.

If I had taken my share of the responsibility, if I had been any kind of a mother, I would have seen to it that there was something to take the place of that nonexistent insurance. And if I had known then what I know now about grief and bereavement, I would have taken a very active role in providing a financial backlog. Just a little security would have made my bereavement less frightening. The prospect of bringing up two children all by myself on my salary was terrifying. No figment of a nightmare or an anxiety attack. Fact.

A psychiatrist told me that in his experience money was usually the exacerbating factor in cases of "pathological" grief. It certainly was an "exacerbating factor" in my grief, which, whether pathological or not, was so crippling that I had had to reach out for professional help.

The psychologist whom I consulted helped me understand how my rage and money worries were entwined. She encouraged me to let the anger out, to talk about it, taught me that I need not be ashamed of it. But money was something else. Either you have it or you don't. Or so I thought. How could I rid myself of financial anxieties unless I got married again? And there was no prospect of that.

Here again, it was a matter of perspective.

"What you are telling me," my therapist said, "is that you are suffering from financial insecurity. So are most other people." This really brought me up short. She was not criticizing me. Simply stating a fact. But I was shocked. How self-involved, self-pitying I had become!

"You have no choice about one thing," she told me. "Your husband is dead. That's a fact and you can't alter it.

"But you do have the choice of looking on the debit side or on the credit side of your life. I suggest you count your blessings. You have two healthy children. You have a good job. You're attractive. And you are healthy. You have a lot of friends.

"Now, you can choose to look at your life any way you want, but it seems to me that you have an awful lot going for you."

This matter-of-fact summing up pulled me out of my self-pity. At least for a time. It was another giant step into life on the other side of grief, just as my realization that I did not want to be a lonely goose, to sink into the underground of widowhood had been a step toward reestablishing myself.

Suddenly, I was no longer Lynn Caine, widow and loser. I was Lynn Caine, competent and vital mother of two. It would have been nice to have a financial buffer against the world. But I had something better. I had friends, health, children. And a good job.

I can't stress enough how important my job was to me. It was not simply that it was interesting and paid a salary that enabled me to get along. More than that, it gave structure to my life. I had to get up in the morning, get dressed and get to work. Even at my lowest times, when I was torn apart by anxieties and fears, the very fact of having a job gave me emotional security. I belonged somewhere. No matter how alone I was in the world, I had a place where I belonged. Work to do.

The best single bit of advice I can give to other widows may be—keep your job if you have one, and find one if you don't. Even if you have children that need you, get a job. A part-time job, a volunteer job, anything that will provide you with a routine and stability. A paid job, of course, is preferable, both in terms of the money and of one's attitude toward it. I realize that this may be out of the question for some women, but it is the *regularity* of the job that I want to stress. I am convinced that having to go to work every day and act as if I were fine and on an even emotional keel helped me back to normality. When I was working, I had a respite from my fears, whether real or fantasy.

Slowly I began to develop confidence in myself and get my financial affairs in somewhat better order. I had done so many stupid things—partly because I hadn't known any better, but mostly because of the craziness of widowhood—that it was a slow process.

My first problem was that Martin and I had never discussed money. Just one of those unliberated things, I suppose, going back to the idea that little girls aren't good at math, a self-fulfilling prophecy that encourages financial incompetence. But the fact was that I had never shared any of the real responsibilities of the household. My job? That was just running off to play. I "ran" the household just about the way a little girl plays house. I never even knew how much money Martin earned—or how much it took to run the household.

That move to Hackensack was an object lesson in financial insanity. I simply had not been able to think clearly about money—or anything else—and the move back to New York marked the first step out of my grief-crazed fog. I went to the children's old school and found that scholarships were available. Thanks to the efforts of friends, we moved into a rent-controlled apartment not very far from where we had lived before. How much better off the three of us would have been if I had never got it into my head to move!

During my crazy period, I had made terrible financial mistakes. And that's why I keep repeating my advice to widows: Sit. Be quiet. Don't move. You have to understand that your mind is not working properly. Even though you think it is. Protect yourself from yourself.

I am still very worried about money. The children and I live on my salary and Social Security and that pittance from the Veterans Administration. But I have learned to cope. I have given up most of the luxuries I used to take for granted. I don't have the paper delivered each morning. I've stopped going to the hairdresser once a week. No more steaks and chops, but lots of spaghetti and tuna fish and casseroles, casseroles, casseroles! No more French wines, but once in a while a jug of California wine. No more expensive vacations. No more summer houses.

I know I am better off than most widows. But why should any woman face deprivation and anxiety and financial terror because her husband dies? Women must learn to protect themselves and their children. We must stop playing child wife. That role hasn't been valid for a long time.

21

Contingency Day

There is a lot to be said for those old-fashioned marriage contracts that spell out financial arrangements. The current Women's Lib marriage contracts disappoint me because they devote so much fretful concern to the question of who is going to change the sheets and take the car to be greased and have so little regard for the truly liberating matter of money.

I can't count the times I have said, "If only I had it to do over again . . ." (And, dear God, please spare me that.) But if I did, I would handle myself and my money much differently. Starting from the day we were married.

Actually, it would be expecting too much to have started on our wedding day. But I should have taken steps the moment I discovered I was pregnant. As soon as I knew I was carrying a new life inside me, I should have asked Martin to sit down and discuss the problem of life insurance with me. To provide for our child.

I was so stupid. I literally did not realize that

there were alternatives to life insurance. Did Martin? I imagine he did. He must have. He was a lawyer. And his specialty was bankruptcy. Surely that must teach a man something about the financial realities.

With the benefit of bitter hindsight and experience, I now know there are alternatives. The simplest might have been to build up a bank account for Jon and later for Buffy simply by depositing a fixed sum in the savings bank every week or month. It could have been in my name, or in trust for them, I don't know. But today, I do know enough so that I would seek advice to find out what was wisest.

There was no reason why we could not have done this. I could have deposited my whole salary in that account. We could have lived very comfortably on Martin's earnings. Or we could have deposited that big monthly Veterans Administration check. Three hundred dollars a month from the time Jonny was born until Martin died would have been a very tidy sum. About thirty-five thousand dollars plus interest. Or we could have split it between savings and stocks. There may have been shrewder ways to have provided for my future and that of our children. If we had only had our wits about us.

Then on that hypothetical day when we were discussing life insurance, I would have, should have asked Martin so many other questions. About wills. About investments. About our plans for the future. But I never did any of this. The future—good or bad—was a reality I never faced.

Death and widowhood are among the most shattering realities. Yet we must face them, and it would be easier to do so if we were prepared beforehand. When I wistfully think back about what I "should have" done, I realize that I *could have* done it. Martin and I *could have* provided for that final contingency of death.

Today I know how I would go about it. I would declare a Contingency Day—an annual review of the financial state of the family. And I would like to recommend such a review to every husband and wife. They could discuss steps to be taken if either husband or wife should die in the next twelve months. How much money the surviving spouse and children would have to live on. What changes in life-style would be necessary. Such a discussion, in the natural context of family life, would minimize some of the later trauma of widowhood (keep in mind that statistics show women usually outlive their husbands).

If Martin and I had done this I would have made fewer crazy decisions, because I would have had a guide, a plan to follow, so that grief-addled as I was, there would have been a lifeline of sanity for me to cling to.

To me, Contingency Day is an eminently reasonable concept, but so strong is the death taboo that some people with whom I've discussed the idea find it shocking.

"Oh, I couldn't do that," one woman protested. "I can't begin to imagine life without my husband." Well, I could not imagine life without Martin. But he died. And here I am. The children and I would have been better off if I could have imagined life without him. I don't consider Contingency Day morbid or shocking in any way. It's a matter of love. Of caring. Of responsibility. Of just plain common sense.

After Martin died, a number of friends told me that they had bought insurance for the first time or increased their coverage to a more realistic sum. Two couples made out wills, something they had never gotten around to before. And one man and wife appointed guardians for their eight-year-old twins—in case they were both in an automobile or plane crash or some other disaster that would leave the boys orphaned. But why wait for the death of a friend to shock one into action?

I can understand that some women might hesitate to say, "Let's sit down tonight and talk about what's going to happen to me and the kids if you die." If this is true for you, it may be easier to start off with something like, "You know, I've never made a will." Or, "I just read that every couple should review their wills at five-year intervals." Or simply ask your husband to read this chapter. I know it is hard to talk about death. So approach it in whatever manner is easiest for you. But approach it.

There is always the possibility that your husband will refuse to join in Contingency Day.* It

* For husbands: If you can't bring yourself to participate in Contingency Day and discuss the very realistic issues of how your wife and children will manage in the event of your death, then at least write a letter to and for your wife that will tell her what she needs to know about such things as insurance, pensions, investments, and debts. It should contain everything your wife and lawyer need to know that is not contained in

may make him too uncomfortable. What then? Go ahead and do it on your own. I'm serious. You owe it to yourself, to your children. I wish someone had pushed me into taking this kind of responsibility.

It should be an annual event with its own set date to be most effective—like Christmas, Thanksgiving, birthdays, anniversaries. My preference is a couple's wedding anniversary, simply because husbands and wives who have instituted this annual review report that their discussions heightened the quality of their relationship. They were brought face to face with the fact that their love was finite. They would not have each other forever. Only until death did them part. There was an increased tenderness, a kind of sweet electricity that reinforced those vows to love and to cherish.

It is important to prepare an agenda. Each family has its own very special concerns, problems, hopes, but the essence of the discussions should be the future—and the direst contingency, death. What should you do if your husband dies? How will you and the children get along?

This cannot be covered in a brief half hour of general discussion. Your first session requires advance planning and organization. In fact, I recommend that you consult your lawyer and possibly an accountant. I want to make it clear that although I am much smarter about handling money these days, I am not an expert. Do not take my suggestions

your will. Once you have written the letter, make copies. Attach one to your will. Stash one away in your safe-deposit box. Give one to your wife and encourage her to ask questions about anything that puzzles her.

as instructions that must be followed. Think about them in the context of your own needs. And remember that times change. Very rapidly. You need professional advice to plan ahead. This scares some people, because of the expense. Good advice does cost, but it may be tax deductible and it will eventually pay for itself. Ethical lawyers and accountants will charge ethical fees. Discuss the fee ahead of time. Ask if you can pay it in installments if necessary.

One couple scoffed at the idea of retaining a lawyer and an accountant. "We don't need all that high-powered advice," Dave said.

"No," his wife agreed. "You'd think we were the Rockefellers with lawyers and accountants and his and her wills and all that."

"Yeah," he added. "With us, it's just a matter of my insurance, and a couple of thousand dollars in the bank. We own our house. There's a mortgage, of course. And the car—there are some payments due on that. But if anything happened to me, Anne would get Social Security and the insurance and my pension money."

"Oh," I said, "would she? Does your pension provide survivor's benefits?"

He hesitated. "You know, I'm not sure. I've always thought it did. I'd better check."

"And how about mortgage insurance?" I asked. "Do you carry that?"

"No," he admitted, a little embarrassed.

"Well, I suggest you look into it. It doesn't cost much and the house would be free and clear if something were to happen to you. Anne and the children wouldn't have to sell it."

Both Anne and Dave looked thoughtful. "I guess there's more to this than we thought," he said.

"Yes," Anne said. "I wish you'd find out about that pension of yours. How much will you get when you retire?"

He didn't know. And I had made my point. Their financial affairs were more complex than they thought.

One important area to clarify on Contingency Day is your husband's pension plan—and yours, too, if you work. It's probably not as good as you assume it is. Find out what happens to your husband's pension if he dies. Will you get anything? What if he dies before he retires? Would you get anything then? You should, of course you should. But very few widows do. Very few private-industry plans pay off to widows. Only about 2 to 3 percent of this country's widows get any money at all from their husbands' private-industry pension plans. Half the widows who are sixty-five and over live on less than two thousand dollars a year.*

But pensions are only one item that should be part of Contingency Day discussions. Probably the top priority should go to your wills, and to the executors of those wills. It might be a good idea for you to be the executrix of your husband's will and he the executor of yours. If you can read and write

---

* As background reading, I recommend a paperback book by Ralph Nader and Kate Blackwell, *You and Your Pension.* It's a quick survey of a subject most women don't know enough about.

and do simple arithmetic, if you are well briefed on the family finances, there is no reason you can't act as executrix. And you can save a lot of money, because you won't have to pay executors' fees.

I'm not going to discuss the subject matter of your wills. That is up to you and your lawyer. Just one word of advice: Don't be in awe of your lawyer. You are paying him for his advice. If you have questions, ask them. There is no such thing as a silly question. If you don't know the answer, it's not silly.

Another area that's a must for Contingency Day is insurance. To what extent are you and the children protected right now? Do you have life insurance? Major medical? Mortgage insurance? Do you need more?

If you have children, it might make a lot of sense to take out life insurance on yourself right now. If you were to be widowed, you would want to take out life insurance on yourself to protect your children. Why wait? It's cheaper now. And the premiums for women are lower than for men because of women's longer life expectancy. That's about the only break insurance companies give women.

Most insurance companies treat women as second-class citizens. For instance, it is relatively easy for men to get disability insurance that guarantees them an income if illness or accident prevents them from working. But it is only very recently that women have been granted the right to buy such insurance. Why? Because, the insurance companies say, a woman might fake an illness just to collect the money. And anyway her husband can take care of her.

Unbelievable? No. This is exactly what one insurance agent told a widow who had to go back to work to support her four children—and was refused disability insurance.

These suggestions are just intended to start you thinking. They are not comprehensive. Your lawyer and your accountant will undoubtedly indicate other areas that should be clarified. For instance, what do you know about the family's bank accounts? Stocks? Real estate? Does anyone owe you money? Do you owe anyone money?

One couple told me that they had started a Contingency Day file. It was just a big brown envelope. Every time they saw a magazine article or a newspaper story that seemed to bear on something that should be discussed, they ripped it out and filed it away to discuss on their next Contingency Day.

In her financial primer, *How to Manage Your Money: A Woman's Guide to Investing* (Little, Brown), Elizabeth M. Fowler, *New York Times* financial columnist, wrote, "I don't intend to be lugubrious, but all married women should prepare themselves to be widows, no matter what their age or status in life."

I couldn't agree more. And I'd like to carry her thought just one step further. One of the most loving acts a man can perform is to teach his wife how to be a widow. It might be that Contingency Day would give your husband the opportunity to show how much he loves you.

22

"You'll Get Married Again"

"You're not a woman to live alone," Martin said. "I want very much for you to get married again." He said this in that same hospital room where a few days earlier he had told me, "I'm going to die, darling. . . . The prognosis is zero."

My first reaction was shock. Then I realized that this was generous of Martin. Generous. And thoughtful. And loving. But when our friends started taking me aside and saying, "Don't worry, Lynn. You'll get married again. You're so attractive," it was more than I could bear. I was bombarded with advice to remarry—or, failing that, to take a lover. It began as soon as people learned that Martin had cancer. One of Martin's colleagues, a lawyer whom I knew only casually, came to visit him in the hospital. When he left, I walked him down the corridor to the elevator. He put his arm around my shoulder and said, "Lynn, you must not worry. I know you will remarry. You'll always have someone to take care of you."

I stiffened and moved away from him. What I understood his words to mean was, "Lynn you're just a woman. You can't take care of yourself. Your feelings are not deep. Neither is your love. So any man will do. Any man will be a haven." Was that really what he meant? I think so. But even if it was not, it is what other people meant. And many of them put it far more crudely.

It was not only men. Women also took me aside and encouraged me to get married again as fast as I could. Some said "for the children's sake." Others said "You need someone to support you." All of them stressed "while you still have your looks."

I was horrified. I don't mean to represent myself as naïve or coy. But how could people try to push me into marriage or an affair while all the time Martin was dying a horrible death—day after day after day of pain? How could people ignore the fact that the man I loved, my husband, the father of my children, was dying? How could they suggest that I "look around"?

And after he died, how could they be so merciless? I needed time to grieve. I needed comfort. I needed peace. A husband, a lover could not have given me these. And what kind of wife would I have, could I have made at this time?

No, it was cruel and unfeeling. Well-meaning? Yes, I suppose so. But I wonder. I think there was a quality of smugness in this advice. Of "Look how well off we are. You better hurry up and reinstate yourself in society."

This pressure to remarry, with its implications

that I could not manage on my own and that I would not be acceptable unless I did remarry, was the cruelest "consolation" of all—and the most commonly proffered one. "Don't worry, Lynn. You're bound to remarry." I heard it over and over. What right did these eager advice-givers have to tell me what to do? I was a grown woman, nobody's ward. It hurt me. It made me feel unfaithful. I didn't need this meddling. More than anything else, however, it brought home to me the fact that married women regard widows as a threat, just as they regard divorcées as a threat.

Because of this, the widow develops a wholly different relationship with wives. I became acutely conscious of this when I was commuting to New York from Hackensack. I usually shared a seat with one of my neighbors in the morning. We sat there, reading our papers, saying little more than "Good morning" and "Have a good day." We went our separate ways when the bus arrived at the Manhattan terminal.

One weekend I met his wife at the supermarket. She said with a frozen smile, "You see more of my husband than I do." It was obvious that she didn't like it.

I suppose I should not have expected her to know that I was not interested in men. I had no energy, sexual or otherwise, then. I was so in the grip of my nightmares and early-morning terrors that it was all I could do to get myself to that bus every morning. The only reason I sat beside her husband was that he was one of the few neighbors I had met and I knew that, like me, he didn't want early-morning conversation. Silence was our only bond. I was completely content then to take refuge in the ghetto of widowhood.

But there comes a time, as the widow's numbness leaves her, when she discovers that she is ostracized by our couple-oriented society. When she is yearning for comfort, for companionship, to be included in the world of families where she used to belong so naturally, then she finds that she has been excluded from most of the intimacies of her old friends, the social life she used to take for granted. The little dinner parties, the friendly get-togethers on Sundays, the impulsive "why don't we pack up the kids and go for a picnic" call from old friends.

This is not paranoia on my part. Or on any widow's part. It is "customary" for married women to drop widows socially even if they have been good friends, says Dr. Richard Conroy, a psychiatrist at St. Luke's Hospital in New York City. The widow becomes a competitor, a possible thief of the husband's love.

And so the widow is left in her exile, in that ghetto of unwanted lonely women, the one that I recoiled from so abruptly when I realized how easy it was to sink into this world apart, to live among a community of rejects.

This ostracism can be fantastically cruel. One woman I know lost her husband a year ago. His death was very sudden, a cerebral hemorrhage. Emily and six-year-old Wendy were left with a minimum amount of insurance, a car and some furniture. That was all. Emily had taught before marriage and now she got a job teaching in a private school in New England.

We spent an evening together when she came to New York recently. "How are you doing?" I asked.

"Don't ask," she said. And she didn't smile. "I feel like a pariah, except in the classroom. When I'm teaching, everything is fine. I'm part of the school community. But come four o'clock and forget it. I don't exist."

"What do you mean?"

"I started by reaching out for friends," she told me. "I knew it was up to me to make the effort. I invited my colleagues and their wives or husbands over for supper—two couples at a time—as soon as I got the house in order. And I set up Saturday cookouts for couples who had children so Wendy could meet them.

"But not one couple has invited me back to dinner in the six months that I've been there. One woman asked me over for sherry when her husband was away, but I haven't been included in one of the Friday-night round of dinner parties. Not one.

"And none of the people who came to the cookouts have ever returned that invitation. Not even extended an invitation to Wendy. I thought the small-town environment would be good for her. Secure. Comfortable. And good for me, too. I thought I was sure to make friends. But I'm thinking of moving back to the city. I'm desperately lonely except at work.

"And, you know," she continued, "I don't even

think that any of the women consider me a threat. I'd be flattered if they did. It's just that they don't know what to do about me. I make them uneasy."

Widows have to face up to the fact that they have what sociologist Robert Fulton calls a "spoiled identity." Widows, Fulton explains, "are stigmatized by the death of the ones they loved." It is true. The widow is stigmatized and she has to fight against society's automatic tendency to consider her taboo because her husband is dead. The progression from wife to widow and back to woman is a hard one. It is impossible for some widows and they sink into that lonely ghetto of widowhood until they, too, die.

It is sad that the progression of grief is so much more difficult for widows than for widowers. But there is a reason for it. Men do not think of themselves primarily as husbands and fathers. They have been encouraged to develop their full potential as unique human beings. So when a man becomes a widower it is a truly heartbreaking blow, but it does not spell an end to his whole way of life. He still has his identity, one that has developed through work, through play, through living. Of course men suffer when they lose a beloved wife. From loss of comfort, loss of coddling, loss of companionship. Above all, just as women do, they suffer from loss of love.

But it is easier for men to find love again. It's a matter of statistics. By the time women reach sixty, roughly a third of them are widows, but only a quarter of the men who are sixty are widowed. Not only do men usually marry women who are younger than they are, but women live longer than men. And the older women become, the fewer men there are to go around.

What is the "moral" of all this? I'm afraid the lesson is that women must learn to be more self-sufficient, more whole. Women must prepare themselves to be able to live alone. Because the majority of women will have to, eventually.

I would like to point out that the widow is not the only woman who feels alone and empty. One gynecologist reported in a professional journal, "My practice is full of 40-year-old women who have a rather lonely and empty life." His conclusion was that "their loneliness and emptiness are due to a lack of friendly communications with their husbands who interpret love purely as sex."

This physician's view is shared by many self-pitying women, but not by me. I think there are other reasons why marriage, this cherished pairing, so often leaves women empty, lonely, whether they are wives, widows or divorcées. One talented woman, screenwriter Eleanor Perry (among her credits: *The Diary of a Mad Housewife*), said, "I thought if you were married, you were symbiotically attached to your husband. It wasn't my husband who made me think this way. I did it to myself. I was an absolute squaw."

She realized what she had done when her husband told her that he wanted a divorce. "I realized then," she says, "that I should not have been just a second-class reflection of him."

Yes, we women do it to ourselves. And most of

us don't realize it until we are divorced or widowed.*
If we all respected ourselves more, disciplined ourselves to attain our potentials and entered marriage
as full partners rather than ego-reflectors, I think
that married women would no longer see the widow
as a threat. They would be sure enough of themselves to look on widows as women who have lost
their loves, who need emotional support, who should
be welcomed into the community of couples because
these women need the community—and the community needs them. Margaret Mead has put it in
her customary forthright style. "I think that family
living," she says, "will become increasingly narrow,
cramped and frustrating unless married couples
open the doors of their homes and bring some
singles into their lives." Opening the door of friendship to the widowed, the divorced and the never-
married "would bring a family blessed relief from
the daily repetition of the same themes and the
same controversies through the welcome diversity
of other views and other interests."

This will not occur until married women gain

* But there is change in the social wind. In the June, 1973,
issue of *Commentary*, Sonya Rudikoff discussed the dissolution
of apparently happy marriages. "These ruptures are frequently
initiated by the women themselves. Not for another man or
because their husbands have become involved with other
women; instead it is . . . in the name of freedom and a fuller
development of their personal lives. They may go to graduate
school or law school or finish a bachelor's degree or work, or
simply, in the old phrase, 'find themselves.' They feel op-
pressed, unfulfilled and, although they didn't marry as child
brides and throughout their married lives they exercised great
freedom—thus displaying their distance from 'A Doll's House'
—they do feel the need for self-discovery and freedom. They
live under the aegis of a new vision of life and of themselves,
from which there is no going back."

courage and have enough faith in their own worth to welcome other women as friends. (And until their husbands can see widows as more than sex objects or bores.)

I was hurt, as so many widows are hurt, to realize that a number of my married friends had dropped me. It took time for this to dawn on me, more time that it does for most widows, I suspect. The reason was my job. As publicity manager of a publishing company, I had a very active, business-oriented life. (And this, incidentally, has been a great advantage in another way. I have more opportunity to meet compatible men than most widows do.) But even with my busy life, I slowly learned that I was being left out of all kinds of affairs that I would have been asked to if Martin was alive.

I was really stricken when I found out that a very dear friend had not invited me to her annual Sunday-after-Thanksgiving dinner. This had been a tradition among our little group for a good ten years. There were eight of us, four couples, who always got together for dinner on that Sunday night. The year after Martin died, I wasn't invited. In my naïveté, in my self-centeredness, I thought at first that the dinner had been canceled because the hostess thought I would be too sad. But no, the dinner had been held. Instead of the Caines, another couple had been invited. Lynn Caine, widow, was no longer a desirable dinner guest.

After that I became conscious of being left out of other gatherings of people whom I had always considered good, dear friends. I became rather bitter about it. Oh, they continued to invite me. To large cocktail binges where they paid back a year's accumulation of social debts. To boring dinner parties where they smugly produced an "available" man. A stray. One of nature's losers. At least that's the way they usually struck me. I'd resent it, resent those "available" men who would look me over.

I'd go home after one of these evenings and pace the floor. I'd complain to Martin as if he were there and could hear me. "Look what I'm reduced to," I would demand. "You should have seen that creep tonight!"

And every time I would swear that I would never accept another such invitation again. But then, someone would call, ask me for dinner. "We want you to meet so-and-so," she would say. "He's not married," she would whisper triumphantly. And I would hear myself saying Yes and hating it. Now I have learned—it took two years—to say "No, thank you" when friends and acquaintances trot out the misfits in their social closet for me. I am convinced that if I do meet a good man, a man who would be good for me and the children, we will meet because of mutual interests and not because of the efforts of my married women friends. I may be wrong. But I think I'm right.

In the meantime I am more or less resigned to the existence of that unspoken message that vibrates in the air between the widow and the wife— "Until you are safely remarried, don't expect to see much of us. I don't want you around my husband." The worst part is, the wives are often right. A widow is like Mount Everest to most men. They seem to feel that they have to make her—just because she's there. Even the husbands of old friends.

My first experience with the sexual vulnerability of widowhood bore this out. It was just a few weeks after Martin's death. The man (he was an old friend) called one night and asked if he could drop by for a drink. He was lonely. His wife was out of town. He wanted to see how I was, and how the children were. He had often dropped in casually while Martin was alive, and I told him I would be glad to see him. I let the children stay up so they could spend a little time with him, too. Eventually, they were tucked into bed and I made fresh drinks for the two of us. He pulled me over to him, kissing me and fumbling with the buttons on my sweater. I pushed him away. But he wasn't upset. He smiled at me and said, "Come, Lynn. What are friends for?"

I was furious. His bland assumption of my willingness was bad enough. But making passes at me in my own apartment, with the children liable to come padding down the hall to the bathroom or out to the kitchen for a drink of water, and the lack of any preliminaries so that I would have had a chance to forestall the whole thing struck me as crude. It was unbelievable. I felt as if I had stepped into another world.

Other widows tell me they have had similar experiences. One woman reported, "The first warning I got was from a friend who had been widowed twice. She said to me, 'I may as well tell you that the husbands of your friends and neighbors, the men you'd least expect, are going to make aggressive passes at you.' And she was right. It started about four or five months after my husband died."

I think that is the real shock, "the husbands of your friends and neighbors," although I might have felt better about this man's crude pass if I had thought he truly wanted to comfort me. For the sexual act can be a comfort, a release, a communication.

I remembered a story a widower friend told. When his wife died—and her death had been expected, just as Martin's had been—he was very broken up. The night before the funeral he was so shaken, so sad he didn't know what to do with himself. He was pacing back and forth. He cried. He could not eat. He had not slept.

The telephone rang. It was the wife of a friend. She asked him to come over and have something to eat with her and her husband. He refused.

Then she asked, "May I come over and see you? I don't want you to be alone this evening."

And indeed, he was not alone. After a couple of drinks, she offered to make love with him. "It was marvelous," he told me later. "I found it enormously comforting. It was a long time after my wife died before I became interested in other women at all, but this one sexual episode came at the correct time. I remember thinking that it was as comforting as it must be for a baby to find his mother's breast. I needed comfort, soothing, surcease. And she gave it to me."

"Did you see her again?" I asked him.

"Oh, yes," he said. "But there was never anything between us again. She was in love with her husband. I knew that. She is really one of those Mother Earth people who have to soothe those in distress."

So I don't know. If someone had offered me sexual surcease, had approached me offering comfort rather than seeking conquest, I don't know what my response would have been. I don't think I could have accepted it. But I don't know.

I'm glad my friend the widower accepted the comfort, and that he had no guilt about it. Because we, the living, must get up and go about our lives. And God knows that's no easy job. We need all the comforting we can get.

23

The Trouble With Love Affairs

The sex urge is part of the life urge. And it slowly came back. As I overcame my anxiety attacks, my terrors, as I worked through my grief, there was a buildup of sexual tension. I was wary. I didn't want a procession of affairs. I wanted a "relationship." I began to think that I would welcome marriage, that now I was ready for it. After all, Martin had told me that was what he wanted for me.

There came a time, almost two years after Martin's death, when I met a man I really liked. He was married. I knew it. But I made a deal with myself—if a relationship were to spring up between the two of us, it would have nothing to do with his marriage. I was not going to be a marriage-breaker. I was a big girl and could handle an affair.

He was a lawyer, a tax specialist who lived in Washington, but he kept a studio apartment in Brooklyn Heights, just across the harbor from the Wall Street headquarters of his firm, and he usually spent one or two days a week in New York. We used to meet for lunch. Then for drinks after work. We progressed to long, flirtatious dinners. I enjoyed it all immensely. I was being courted, and I loved it. Here was a man who cared for me, who was wooing me. There was a sexual attraction. There was also that hint of forbidden fruit.

One night as he dropped me off at my apartment after dinner, he said, "Next week, you're coming to my place. I want you to see it. I'll cook and we can take our shoes off and listen to music and look at my view of the harbor."

I can't really explain why I was so excited. But I was. And nervous and upset. I was serious about this man. I thought about him a lot. And I thought about making love with him. But I was worried. I feared rejection. My body worried me. My figure was all right, but Jonny had been born by Caesarean section and I had a long, deep scar on my belly. Martin had loved that scar. To him, it meant his son. But to a stranger, I feared it might seem disfiguring. And my thighs. They weren't as firm as they had been when I was twenty-one. Or when I was thirty-one. With a husband, it doesn't matter. He sees you as you used to be. And you both accept the inroads of time on each other's bodies. But a lover?

I laughed. Here I was, at last, thinking of taking a lover. I was delighted. Nervous, yes. Fearful of rejection, yes. But not really believing I would be rejected. It was like one of those delicious worries you make up for yourself just to enhance suspense.

I arrived a considerate ten minutes late. The view was marvelous, just as he had promised. He was playing Mozart—one of my favorites. But once the entrance flurry was over, I was terribly uneasy. When Tom (that's not his name) gave me my drink, my hand shook.

"You're nervous, aren't you?" he asked concernedly. "It's the first time you've been in a man's apartment since . . . ?" I nodded and gulped down my vodka martini. I was truly confused. I know, looking back, that I was still in my crazy period. I wasn't emotionally sturdy enough to handle an affair—no matter what I thought. But I didn't know that then.

I had several vodka martinis. I was so nervous I didn't realize how much I was drinking, and when it came time to eat, I could barely force down a couple of forkfuls.

"You're still nervous?" Tom asked.

"Yes," I laughed. And I could hear the brittle edge to the laughter. "I think I need some more vodka."

He gave me a few drops. I know he didn't want to. I forced down a bit more food. And then we made love.

That's the wrong expression. We didn't make love. We grappled with each other. I suspect that neither of us had understood what the other expected from the evening. I think Tom had wanted to show off his bachelor pad, to listen to music and perhaps to sit, hold hands and kiss. To kiss and admire the view of the harbor. I don't think he ever wanted more than a tender playing-with-fire relationship. He was not a man to be unfaithful in fact.

But I had had a love affair in mind. I had no patience with kisses. I wanted sex. Intercourse. The mix of guilt and grief, vodka and desire blinded me to his feelings. All I was aware of were my own needs. Tom, I am sure, was confused by the turn I insisted on giving the evening.

And it was a disaster. He couldn't. No matter how I tried I could not stir him. It was an abortive, sweaty, strained interlude. And then—I had to rush to the bathroom. I was sick to my stomach. Too much vodka, too little food. Too much emotion, too little satisfaction.

Tom was appalled, but courteous, considerate. He made me lie down. He sponged off my sweaty face. And finally, he helped me gather those bits of clothing here and there on the floor. He combed my hair and took me home. We didn't talk. I thanked him as I got out of the car. "I'm sorry," I said and went blindly into the elevator, into the apartment and into my bed. The bed I had shared with Martin. I was sick. Really sick. The vomiting was over. This sickness was in my bones, in my head, in my soul. "What the hell are you doing to yourself, Lynn Caine?" I asked. "What would Martin think?" And fell asleep before I could frame an answer.

The next morning, struggling with my vodka hangover, I realized I had left my glasses at Tom's place. I couldn't call him. Just couldn't. But that afternoon, when I returned to the office after lunch the receptionist handed me a little package. My glasses, and a note from Tom: "I hope you're feeling better." We had lunch a couple of weeks later—

just to prove how civilized we were, I guess. And that was the end of that.

So much for affairs, I told myself. That sex appeal of yours, I said, is not that appealing. Stop fooling yourself. You are a middle-aged mother with two children. Act like it.

But sexuality was creeping back into my life. As I emerged from grief, I began to feel more and more aware. I wanted sex. After all, it had been an integral and enjoyable part of my adult life.

But what was I to do? I did what every woman probably does—I masturbated. Yet I felt frantically guilty about it. So guilty that I never let Martin, who represented the "good" part of my life, enter my masturbatory fantasies. It was always someone I had seen or heard about or read about—never anyone I knew. Never anyone I had met. When I told the psychologist about this, I think she was appalled that a woman of my supposed intelligence still thought masturbation was wrong. She encouraged me. Explained over and over again how normal it was. But it didn't help. I think I had been too well programmed when I was young to be able to change my feelings about self-stimulation. I didn't like it. I resented my need. Sometimes I blamed Martin for having put me in such a bind.

Masturbation was no substitute for a sex life. But it did dissipate some of that sexual tension. And it reinforced my knowledge of myself as a sexual being.

Some months later, I met a man who needed me as much as I needed him. He was a painter— fairly successful, but penniless for all that. I'll call him Richard. He had had an unhappy marriage. His divorce had left him feeling bruised and inadequate. Between us, the accent had been on friendship, on shared interests, not on sex. He had been one of the wonderfully perceptive men who realized that Jonny needed men in his life, and he used to appear on Saturdays to take him out to toss a football around in the park or to go bicycling. And when they came home, clear-eyed and fresh-air rosy, Richard and I would have a drink, then Buffy would snuggle in his lap while he read her a story and I cooked Saturday-night supper for the four of us.

It was easy and informal. Looking back, I suppose we were two emotional cripples, supporting each other as best we could. And I think we were successful—up to a point. For me, just having a man around the house to help me carry stuff home from the supermarket, a man to go to the movies with, a man who was gentle with the children as well as with me was immensely comforting and fulfilling. It more than made up for the lack of excitement in our relationship.

But Richard had his problems, just as I had mine, and our relationship began to fray almost from the start. His problem was an ego that had been battered. He wanted more love than I had to give. More time than I had to give. He resented the time I spent with the children. He began to see them as rivals, and the wonderful rapport he had established with them disintegrated. He told Buffy she was babyish; he told Jonny he was fresh, and the children withdrew into themselves. It was a bad time. We began to bicker. Then to fight.

Our sex life went from mediocre to rotten immediately. Sex, in fact, had always been a problem for us—because of the children. That's one of the troubles with love affairs.

It's a housing problem. If you have children, you have to go to his apartment or to a hotel. You can't have him spend the night. It's not good for the children. So you go to his apartment. And that's not so great either. After seventeen years of marriage I was spoiled. First of all, Richard's place was drab, uncomfortable, cold. It was a painter's studio rather than an apartment. The bed was a mattress in a corner. And we were not young lovers. I missed the comfort, the very warmth, of my own apartment.

I'd fall asleep after lovemaking. Then I'd wake up. What time is it? It's still dark out. I can sleep a little longer. I would sleep fitfully off and on all night putting off the moment of misery. But finally, just before dawn—up. I had to get up.

There was the business of getting dressed all over again. Should I take a shower? Or skip it? Pulling on the stockings I'd worn all day, now disgustingly loose and baggy. By the time I was ready to leave, I felt like the end of beyond. And I looked it. Prickly-eyed. Sallow. Yawning.

Then there was the problem of getting a taxi in those predawn hours. Richard would pull on a pair of jeans, shrug into his raincoat and pad down with me, yawning and whiskery. I was always embarrassed. I was sure the cab drivers knew just what I'd been up to. And they probably did.

I would huddle in a corner of the cab and then—into the house past the yawning doorman. Out of my clothes again. I would crave a bath or a shower, but I didn't want to wake the children or my mother. Into bed. Too awake to go to sleep. Finally I would doze off. And minutes later the alarm would ring. It was terrible. If anyone were to ask me about the wages of sin, my answer would have to do with getting up in the middle of the night, getting dressed and going home.

There was more and more dissonance between us. Richard's attitude toward the children. My impatience. His increasing demands. My own changing feelings about the man-woman relationship. And, of course, the basic lack of commitment. Our neuroses no longer meshed. They clashed and jangled.

No matter how we tried to disguise this, we were both aware of it. The final episode was like a second honeymoon gone wrong. It was school vacation. My mother took the children to visit friends in the country for a week. Richard and I would have the apartment to ourselves. We could "play house." No more waking up in the middle of the night and taxiing home. We could make love and fall asleep until morning—just like real people.

I told myself that this would make all the difference. We were cranky with each other because there were too many pressures on us, too many other people to consider. Now, for once, we could be alone with each other. But somehow it just did not work. Some nights dinner was too late for him.

He played the phonograph too loud. Picky little things. It was a disappointing interlude.

We saw each other a few more times after this week. But the dissonance between us increased. Finally, one Sunday afternoon in his dreary apartment when I should have been home with the children, I asked myself, "What in the world are you doing here? He's a pain in the neck. You're not having any fun. You're not in love with him, nor he with you. He's not even very good in bed. You're too good for him," I told myself. I went home twenty minutes later. Jon and Buff needed me. More than he needed me. More than I needed him. And that really was the end.

I learned a lot from this first significant relationship with a man since I had become a widow. A lot about myself and how I had changed. I had become much more independent without even suspecting it. Some of this may have been due to the ferment of Women's Lib. I wasn't active, but I was sympathetic. Consciousness-raising was in the very atmosphere. My feelings about the kind of relationship I wanted with men had changed in the years since Martin had died. I did not need a man for my own self-esteem any longer. And in a very strange way, this made me much less lonely. I no longer worried about whether or not a man—or a woman—liked me. My concern was with how I liked them, how they affected me, what kind of people they were. I no longer sought approval. I discovered that I was happy enough alone, governing my own life. And I've modified that purposely. I am not "happy." But I am "happy enough." I am often lonely. I know what I am missing, but I can cope with life now. I find more pleasure in solitude. I am becoming a more serious woman. I want to write. I want to savor my children. I seek delight, but my delights are different now.

This change in me, I am sure, was one of the forces at work in the relationship with Richard that brought it to an end. I wanted to be a partner, and I wanted my partner to pull his own weight. As long as I played mummy, nanny, housekeeper and mistress, Richard relished it. But when I began to assert myself, want some coddling myself, he didn't like it. He accused me of wanting to drain him dry—exactly what I thought he had been doing to me.

I had come a long way from the grief-wracked woman who had been so shocked by an abortive sexual overture from the husband of a friend three years earlier. Now I would simply have laughed it off.

No, if I were to have another man in my life, it would have to be a completely different relationship. For one short evening, I thought I had found it. With a younger man. Other women had talked to me about their experiences with younger men. Women's magazines had begun to point out that relationships between younger men and older women could be mutually rewarding. Psychiatrists and physicians had reported that the sex drive of a woman in her forties was more compatible with that of a man in his thirties than with one in his forties. It made sense to me—until I met a younger man who attracted me.

He was a journalist. We met at a cocktail party and had an instant rapport. He suggested we have dinner together. We did. We shared a steak, a bottle of wine and a lot of that semi-psychoanalytic talk that new acquaintances revel in. We were exchanging life stories when he confided, "I was four years old before I ever laid eyes on my father."

"How come?" I asked.

"He was in the war," he replied matter-of-factly.

Suddenly I realized that this man was much younger than I. I've never been good at arithmetic, but it was easy to figure out that he must have been born in 1941 or 1942—and I was born a generous decade earlier. As we talked, I discovered that we perceived life differently, laughed at different things, quoted different popular songs, had different memories.

But I found him attractive. Very attractive. And when we left the restaurant, "Come on, let me show you my place," he coaxed. But I said no. It wasn't moral scruples. It wasn't that I didn't want to. It was vanity. I had that Caesarean scar road-mapping my stomach. And I hadn't shaved my legs in days. I didn't want him to compare me unfavorably to the young girls I was sure he had. So I said no and meant it—even though I regretted it a bit. He was terribly attractive, but I was concerned with emotional hangovers. I didn't want to be hurt. I didn't want to be rejected. As I was getting ready for bed that night, I scoffed at myself for my cowardice. "You're supposed to be liberated," I told myself. But then, true liberation may simply be feeling free to say no—no matter what your reasons are.

Perhaps nature has some perverse quirk and insists on suffering as a prerequisite of growth. It has been true with me. The ability to say no represents growth as well as liberation for me. I have more confidence in myself, more faith in others. I have a new perspective on life.

A colleague told me a story about Isaac Bashevis Singer that illustrates the kind of perspective I mean. Years ago, when he was not the successful author he is today, my colleague telephoned him.

"I have good news for you," she said.

"What is this good news?" Mr. Singer asked.

"I sold your three short stories!"

There was a pause.

"I'm sorry," the writer said, "there are only two stories." He had given one to a small literary magazine that could not afford to pay him.

My friend gasped. "Mr. Singer, that's a catastrophe!"

"No. No, my dear," he said. "It is not a catastrophe. Little children wouldn't die of it."

I think of that story very often. Mr. Singer knew that there is strength in the definition of priorities. One establishes a sense of what is important and what is trivial. Would little children die of it?

Today I ask myself this question a lot. Sometimes I rephrase it. Would little children benefit from it? For when you come right down to the bedrock of sexual relationships, of emotional relationships, of that rarity called love—for a widow, it's the children who are all-important. I have a great sense of responsibility toward Buffy and Jonny. If they are to grow up to be emotionally mature and healthy, I have to provide the right kind of home environment. Any man with whom I want to have a relationship, a serious relationship, must be able to establish a rapport with my son and my daughter. He must be able to be warm with them, to be tender. To care for them. To care enough to put himself second at times.

I know that if I ever do find this kind of man, he will more than likely have children of his own. He will probably be a widower or a divorcé. And that means there will be all kinds of adjustments to be made. My adjustments to him and to his children. His to me and to my children. And the adjustments of his children to my children. And I sometimes wonder how Jon and Buff would feel if I were to mother and love other children.

It is far more complicated than I ever dreamed it would be in those early days of widowhood when people were so certain that they were doing the right thing when they encouraged me to remarry.

I have had a good marriage. And I won't settle for anything less. Sex? Ah, that's another question. I'm not a woman to live happily without sex. But I have learned that I can.

It is not easy to be a widow. These days, I think that I am braver and more confident. But when I come home from a date and I shut my door and I'm alone at night—I really don't feel so brave. I'm lonely. Going out with men accentuates the loneliness of not being married. I can face loneliness now, that kind of loneliness. But that doesn't stop it from hurting.

Part Four

CHILDREN GRIEVE, TOO

24

"Does My Daddy Know I'm in First Grade?"

I knew that Buffy and Jonny missed their father terribly, but at the beginning I did not realize how much. And what I did not understand and what nobody told me was that children have to work through their grief, too. When they were babies, I read dozens of books on child care, but none of them ever told me anything about helping children cope with the fact of death, helping children accept the death of a parent. This should be changed. Children need to learn about death. Children—and their parents—must be helped to understand that death is the price of life. Those people who pretend that the death of a goldfish can teach little children about death are refusing to face reality. The death of a goldfish and the death of a father? Oh, no. That is no equation.

What would I have done differently, knowing what I know now? One thing I wish I had done is draw the children out more. I should have talked to them more about how I missed their father, just as Martin and I should have talked to them more openly and honestly and at length about his illness.

If I had confided in them how much I missed Martin, if I had told them how terrible I felt after Martin died and during those months in Hackensack, it might have allowed them to make some contact with how terrible they felt. They might have been able to talk. But I didn't show them my fears; on the other hand, I never told them everything was rosy. I took it from day to day and tried to upset them as little as possible. I was actually trying to spare myself. If I let these floodgates down, everything will fall apart, I thought. I couldn't take the chance. I suppose I should have said, "I am so frightened. I am so lonely. Isn't it rotten here without Daddy?" But at the time, I couldn't.

Jon found it very difficult to accept his father's death, and I only became aware of this after Martin had been dead for six months. In Hackensack, I overheard a boy ask him, "Why doesn't your mother have a car?"

Jon said, "Because she can't drive. That's why."

Then the boy asked, "Well, can't your father drive?" And Jon didn't say anything. I waited and I saw that he had that closed, tight look on his face that meant he was frightened and embarrassed.

I spoke up. "Jon's father is dead," I told the boy.

Buffy did not fall into this denial pattern, but she was very confused. It was all very unsettling for a little girl. One morning, more than a year after Martin died, Buffy came wandering into the kitchen where I was getting breakfast. She was half dressed, her hairbrush in her hand.

"Mamma," she asked, "does my daddy know I'm in first grade now?"

How do you answer a question like that? I didn't know how to handle it. What should I say? The question hung there. Why does she have to ask me first thing in the morning when my head is filled with cotton?

The answer was obvious. If Buffy's daddy knew that she was in first grade, he wouldn't be dead. If he had any consciousness at all, he would not be dead. There is no consciousness past death. I couldn't let Buffy think that.

"No, Buffy," I said. "Daddy is dead. He doesn't know you are in the first grade now. But if he did know, he'd be very pleased."

"Yes, I think so," Buffy said. "He'd be glad I'm learning to read." And she went back to brushing her hair for school.

What else went through her mind? Was this answer enough? I don't know. You can't pry into a child's head and heart. You can only guess. Only rely on your own heart and intuition.

I worry about Buffy. Martin's death may have been more of a blow to her than to Jon, because Buffy was too young to have verbalized her feelings as she might have at an older age. I often worry that Buffy may never dare love anyone for fear that person will die, too.* Or leave her alone. I try

* Dr. Gilbert Kliman, a child psychiatrist who specializes in helping children master childhood traumas like death and divorce, says that the death of a father may have a delayed effect on children if they are not helped to express their feelings about it. One effect may be that the child becomes afraid to love. The youngster worries that if he or she dares to love another person, that person, too, may be taken away from them.

hard to reassure her about this. Because I love my little daughter very much.

When she was little, one of her greatest delights was to have Martin hoist her up to his shoulder and prance around the room with her. She would clutch his head and beam. Until just a few months ago, whenever she met a man she would ask him to put her up on his shoulder "like my daddy used to do." Buffy is very conscious of the hole left in her life by Martin's death.

She yearns for a father. Even now, at eight, she still asks almost every man who comes to the house, "May I call you Daddy? I wish you were my daddy." There is such a hunger in her for a daddy, a father to call her own.

But it is not all sweetly unconscious pathos. Buffy, like all children, is a beguilingly shrewd little operator. Not too long ago we were in the supermarket, trudging up and down the aisles with our cart. A young man was standing in front of the fruit-counter scale waiting for his purchase to be weighed. Buffy went up to him and asked, "May I call you Daddy?" I was so embarrassed I wanted to disappear.

The man was obviously taken aback, but he smiled and said, "Of course, if you'd like to." Buffy pursued her advantage. "Well, then," she asked, "will you give me a quarter?" I couldn't stop myself from laughing even as I scolded her. But at the same time, this kind of thing worries me.

And she does have an enormous craving for love. When friends of ours visited one Sunday afternoon, Buffy snuggled up to the wife and said,

"Why don't you have a little girl?" Buffy didn't wait for an answer. "You could adopt me, if you want," she offered.

I was shaken. Did Buffy feel she was up for grabs? That there was no stability in her life? I don't know the answers to these questions. And I certainly didn't stop to worry them out then and there.

"Do you think I'd give you away to anybody?" I asked Buffy indignantly. "Do you think I could get along without you? You're my little girl and I love you a lot. Nobody else can have my Buffy." That seemed to reassure her. She still snuggled up to my friend, but she has never offered herself for adoption again.

I tossed and turned that night. Worrying. Reproaching myself. What could I do to make Buffy feel as wanted, loved and needed as she is?

I make a point of spending as much time as I can with Buffy now. I keep telling her that I want to spend more, but she knows that I have to work and that our time is necessarily limited. I think that this honesty helps. One evening I came home from work to find Buffy alone in her room crying. My mother said she didn't know what was wrong with her.

"What's the matter, Buff?" I asked as I picked her up and cuddled her. "What's wrong with my girl?"

Buffy snuggled as close as she could get and said, "I need love."

"I know," I said. "And you have to tell me when you need extra love. I love you all the time. You know that. But it's hard when a little girl and her mother don't have a lot of time together, isn't it?"

"Uhhuh," sniffed Buffy.

"Now, here's what, Buffy," I said. "You have to tell me every time you need a little extra love. You just come and tell me. All right?"

She does, and it seems to have made a big difference. Sometimes when I come home from work at night, Buffy will follow me to my room while I change and say, "Mamma, I need love." And we'll snuggle and we'll talk and she seems to feel happy about the fact that she can ask for extra attention and get it.

25

"I Miss My Father So Much"

Bringing up children all by myself is difficult. And a frightening responsibility. It's hard to be both mother and father. Jon needs a father. He needs a man in his life. Living with his mother, his sister and his grandmother puts him in an overwhelmingly female environment. And he needs a father to discipline him. When Martin was alive, all he had to do was say "Jon" in a certain no-nonsense tone and Jonny stopped whatever he was up to and behaved as he should. But I find myself screaming at him when he doesn't do his homework or pick up his room or come home on time. And my screaming has very little effect. I'm fortunate that he is such a good boy because otherwise, without a man, I don't know how I could manage.

There are other difficulties in being a single parent. Other widows know them only too well. The unbearable loneliness of holidays. Christmas. Without a father to help trim the tree, to share secrets with, it's just not the same holiday. And birthdays lose their savor without a father. There is a whole lopsided quality to family life, no matter how well we manage.

I long so much to be able to share the children with Martin. The problems. And the joys. Because there are joys. We are a happy family again. We are very close these days.

I make a point of seeing that we do as many things as we can together—chores as well as pleasures. In the evening, I'll read to Buffy while Jon works on one of his projects in the same room. Or Jon, who has a great imagination, will make up a story for us. Or we watch television. Sometimes we cook together. The important thing, I have discovered, is just being there and being involved with them.

I feel it is very important for them to know that I am human. That I worry, that I have faults, that I try hard and sometimes fail. That I love them, yet sometimes get annoyed with them. I don't want them to put me on any pedestal. I don't belong there.

As a result, I get a lot of back talk from them. I try to respond with dignity but without being pompous. A lot of times, they complain about me. "You're not like a mother," Jonny told me once.

"What do you mean?"

"I don't know, but you're not like other kids' mothers. You're always doing something and you talk to us as if we were grown up."

"Well, did you ever stop to think that you are not like other kids?" I asked. "You're my kids. And I'm your mother. And we have a good time together. Isn't that all that matters?"

Jon seemed to accept that. At least for the moment. I know that a time is coming when they will feel they have to rebel against me. But I hope their adolescent rebellion won't be too harsh. They already demonstrate a lot of independence. There are times, and I have learned to treasure them, when all they want is to be home and quiet with me. But they are both outgoing children and have a lot of friends. One thing I don't worry about is either one of them being tied to my apron strings.

I'm often amazed, in fact, at the extent of their independence. One morning after Jon had left for school, he came back just as I was walking out the door on my way to work.

"What are you doing back here?" I asked.

"I forgot my mugging money," Jon said.

"Your what?"

"My mugging money. Mamma," he explained, "every day I take a quarter to school in case I get mugged."

"What do you mean?" I asked, stunned.

"Well, when these tough kids come along and start hassling me, I just throw my money on the sidewalk and run. I can run fast and by the time they have picked up the quarter, I'm safe.

"If I didn't have any mugging money," he said, "they'd beat me up."

I was frightened. "I'm going to walk you to school," I said.

Jon was horrified. He wouldn't hear of it. "I'm not a baby. Everyone would laugh at me if you walked me to school. Stop worrying," he said paternally. "I know how to take care of myself." My young man of the world!

Sometimes I forget that he is still a child, a child who misses his father very much—and finds it hard to express his feelings. This was brought home to me when his fifth-grade teacher called me in for a consultation. Jon had been acting up in school.

Jon was present at our meeting. He denied misbehaving. He said he had not been obstreperous. "Jon," I said, "no one is making anything up. Your teacher asked me to come in so the three of us could discuss it. We want to find out why you are acting this way. Then we can help you control yourself better."

Jon whipped around and out of the conference room. Then he came back and said in a tight, high voice, "I miss my father so much on weekends when he used to play football with me and talk and everything." And then he ran out of the room again. He was crying.

This was the first time that Jon had said anything, anything at all, about missing his father. He had talked about Martin, the things they used to do together, but he had never before been able to come out and say it—that he missed him very much.

There had been clues before that Jonny was upset, but I had not recognized them. I didn't know enough about the process of grief to pick them up and act on them. For instance, Jon had suffered from the same kind of irrational anger and anxieties that I had. But I only understood this many months after Martin died, when the father of one of Jon's classmates was killed in a tragic accident, the victim of a drunken driver. This got Jon frantically stirred up. The day after the funeral, he said furiously, "I don't want to go to school today. I hate Liz. I'm not going to talk to her. Just because her father died. I don't care."

I suddenly realized that this death was very frightening to him and brought him face to face with thoughts and fears that he had been bottling up. I made a point of spending some special time with him just as I had with Buffy and encouraging him to talk. It was difficult. Jonny resisted talking about his feelings, but he managed to tell me how he hated to tell other children that his father was dead. It embarrassed him and it also made him angry, just because he was embarrassed. And it turned out that he worried a lot about what would happen if I got sick or lost my job. It would probably have been easier if I had encouraged him to talk two years earlier. But I didn't know enough to do it. I hope that little by little he will be able to get rid of all the grief and bewilderment that's inside him so it won't boil up in later adolescence.

He is getting a lot better about discussing things that are on his mind. Recently, he found an opportunity to interview the actor and writer Anthony Quinn for his school paper, *The Blue Star*. It was quite an interview. Jon took along his tape recorder and later, when he first played the tape for me, I was amazed at the direction Jon had given the interview. He started off, "Mr. Quinn, do you think that if you were a child and your father hadn't died and if you were rich, would you be a different person now?"

There they were—the two things that had been haunting Jon's life—the death of his father and my constant worries about money.

Mr. Quinn handled it beautifully.

"Every boy," he told Jon, "tries to emulate his father in some ways and eventually be better than his father. Probably the tragedy of my life was that my father died and I had nobody to look up to.

"So as I grew up, I made imaginary heroes for myself. Like great writers and great painters. Even great athletes. But very few ever really measured up to what I felt about my father.

"And, of course, if I had been rich," he continued, "my life would have been different because my drives would have been different. When food and clothes and all the essentials come too easily, I think that a boy is liable to have great emotional troubles later. Simply because he never got a chance to appreciate the very simple necessities of life. Once you have been as poor as I was, even buying a pair of shoes is still an event for me. I don't take it for granted."

Jon got a lot of compliments when his interview appeared in the paper. It was a great success. But an even greater success, I thought, was Jon's ability to ask questions that helped himself.

Both Buffy and Jon have developed tremendously in the past year. They constantly startle me with their courage, their intuition, their emotional strength. And there was a period last year when they had to muster all their strength.

There was an echo of catastrophe. A lump in my breast. The surgeon said "a serious lesion." It had a "somewhat ominous shape."

How do you tell the children that Mamma, too, may have cancer? That Mamma, too, is going off to the hospital for a "little operation" to remove a "little lump" from her breast? Jon was almost twelve and Buffy was "half past seven." They were smart, shrewd youngsters, not the protected little children of three years ago who sat there, uncomprehending, as Martin explained that he would be in and out of the hospital a lot. Now I had to tell them the truth.

But I couldn't! I couldn't. I had the horrors at night. Told myself I had to tell them first thing in the morning. But in the morning, I felt gray and tired and decided to tell them in the evening. A day went by. Two days. Finally I couldn't wait any longer.

"Look," I began desperately, "I'm going to the hospital Tuesday morning for a little operation. A cyst," I explained, avoiding saying "a lump on my breast."

"Where is it?" Jon asked.

"What's a cyst?" Buffy asked.

"It's on my breast," I told them. "Right here. A cyst is something like a pimple."

Jonny said, "I think you're hiding something from us."

I went cold. How did he know? How did he *know!* Lynn Caine, you are an idiot, I told myself. Jon and Buffy can read. They see all those ads and posters about the ten signs of cancer. They watch soap operas in the afternoon with their grand-mother. They know. They know!

"You're right," I said. "Sometimes these cysts are malignant. Cancerous. I won't know until the doctor has taken it out and examined it."

Jon's eyes went far away. Buffy started wrig-gling around. "Mama, can I call Maria and see if she can come over to play?"

"Sure, ask her if she wants to stay for lunch," I said. It was Saturday. We might as well have a good, normal day. As good as we could. I knew Jon was disturbed. But at least this time I had told them the truth. I couldn't give myself much credit for it, however. They had forced it out of me.

Buffy had danced off to the telephone in her quicksilver way. No problem with that one, I thought. But Jon? He was still sitting there, looking off into space, his eyes not focusing on anything. He has to think it through, I told myself.

Then, cut it out. You're evading again. I thought you had promised yourself that "next time" and "if I had to do it over again" and all that, you would talk to the children, help them get in touch with their feelings. And you're not. You're just letting Jonny slide over it again. Letting it all accu-mulate inside him—like some monstrous cancerous cyst full of fear!

I sat down beside Jon. "No fun, huh, Jonny?" I had to force the words out. I felt tongue-tied. Had Martin felt this way? Had he? Oh, poor Martin! Screw it! It's poor Jonny right now. Jonathan Caine, orphan. That's what he is thinking.

"Jon, it's tough," I finally got out. "I'm worried.

It might be cancer. But, you know, not all cancer kills. This is a cancer that's more or less on the surface. The doctor scoops out the cyst, just the way I scoop out melon balls." I tried to laugh, but it was more like a sob. "Even if it is cancer, Johnny, it won't kill me. There is a lot the doctors can do. I promise you.

"I suppose you're wondering what would happen to you if something awful happened to me?"

Jon nodded.

I put my arm around him and that going-on-twelve boy snuggled up to me like a five-year-old. "Do you remember when Daddy was sick and one day you were taking a bath and you asked me what would become of us if Daddy died?"

He nodded.

"Do you remember that I told you we would be very sad for a very long time, but then we would be happy, because we're basically happy people? Well, we're happy again, aren't we? And I did take care of you just the way I promised you I would. And I can tell you that if Daddy were alive today, he'd be very proud of you.

"Now, if anything should happen to me, if this rotten, lousy cyst turns out to be cancerous, I promise you it won't be like Daddy's. You can talk to the doctor about it and he'll tell you I'm right. He'll operate on it. And I will go back to work. And we'll go on living just the way we've been living. Sometimes I'll be mad at you and scream at you and sometimes I'll be too tired to talk to you, but all the time I'll love you and all the time I'll take care of you.

"If it is cancer, I'll have to go see the doctor every few months for a checkup. And if it should get worse, he'll have to do another operation, perhaps. But I won't be in any pain. I can still go to work. We can still be together. And this can be cured." (Was my explanation less than honest? The statistics on breast cancer are not all that rosy. All I can say is that I was as honest as I could be.)

I don't know what else I said, but I kept going on and on until Jon relaxed enough to start asking questions.

In the middle of the night, Buffy came crawling into my bed. "I had a bad dream," she sniffled. "And I don't feel so good."

"Oh, poor Buffy. Come here," and I cuddled her and wiped away the tears and blew her nose as if she were two years old. "Now, tell me, where don't you feel so good?"

"I hurt inside my body," she whimpered.

"Here?" And touched her stomach.

"No."

"Here?" and I felt her forehead.

"No."

"Here?" And I pulled her big toe.

"No," she said and started smiling. Then she stopped. "I'm frightened. I don't want you to go to the hospital. I want you to stay here with us."

"Oh, Buffy," I said, "I know what's making you feel bad. You are afraid I'll be like Daddy."

She nodded, just as Jon had nodded that morning. I pushed up the pillows and sat up and put her in my lap. "Buffy, it won't be like Daddy. I promise you. There are all kinds of cancer, just like there are all kinds of colds. You know, sometimes you have the sneezes and sometimes you have the coughs and sometimes you just have a bad sore throat . . . and some of them are bad and some aren't so bad. And Buffy, we don't even know if it's cancer. The doctor is going to find out so that he can make me well if it is."

"The doctor can't make you well," Buffy objected.

"Oh, yes, he can," I assured her. "This is a different kind of cancer. I told Jon all about it this morning when you were playing with Maria. And I told him how the doctor can just cut out this cancer and throw the bad part away."

I could feel her tense little body relax. "Come on, let's go to sleep," I said. "We have a lot to do tomorrow."

Three days later, I went to the hospital.

The cyst was benign!

Things are better now. I tell myself the worst is over. Buffy still craves extra-large doses of love and cuddling, but she never hesitates to tell me that she wants love. And Jon seems sunnier and happier these days.

The children are a responsibility. A frightening one. But they are also my bridge to a more stable world. If it hadn't been for the children, I would have had no focus for my life after Martin died. No reason to live. And no love. Perhaps I would never have come to know and love my children quite as much as I do if Martin had not died.

And in some ways, now that the storms of grief are over, I feel closer to Martin than I have for a long time. He once told me, "As long as you are alive, darling, I am alive." I have no mystical feelings—it is simply that I can think about Martin now with love and honest affection. The hate, the anger, have all burned away.

The children and I are able to talk about him more easily. With regret. With sadness. But with love. Sometimes they feel sorry for themselves that they have only one parent. At those times I tell them, "Look, you have one terrific parent. Some kids just have two yukky parents. So stop feeling sorry for yourselves." I say this, because at least it is positive.

But as of today (and I cross my fingers), our family seems to work as a family. The children get along well with each other and with their friends. They are, I think, extraordinarily well behaved. Perhaps a little too responsible, too grown up for their years. But when I start worrying about this, I tell myself that it is better than being irresponsible and immature.

And they face life with courage. They are impatient with subterfuges. A few weeks ago, Jon overheard a guest saying that his mother had "passed away." When he left, Jon asked me what "passed away" meant.

"It means died," I told him.

"Why didn't he say so?" asked Jon.

Why not, indeed?

Part Five

A DIFFERENT WOMAN

"Widow" is a harsh and hurtful word. It comes from the Sanskrit and it means "empty." I have been empty too long. I do not want to be pigeon-holed as a widow. I am a woman whose husband has died, yes. But not a second-class citizen, not a lonely goose. I am a mother and a working woman and a friend and a sexual woman and a laughing woman and a concerned woman and a vital woman. I am a person. I resent what the term widow has come to mean. I am alive. I am part of the world.

If fate had reversed its whim and taken me instead of Martin, I would expect him to be very much part of the world. I cannot see him with the good gray tag of "widower." He would not stand for it for one moment. And neither will I. Not anymore.

But what of love? The warmth, the tenderness, the passion I had for Martin? Am I rejecting that, too?

Ah, that is the very definition of bereavement.

WIDOW

The love object is lost. And love without its object shrivels like a flower betrayed by an early frost. How can we live without it? Without love? Without its total commitment? This explains the passionate grief of widowhood. Grief is as much a lament for the end of love as anything else.

Acceptance finally comes. And with it comes peace. Today I carry the scars of my bitter grief. In a way I look upon them as battle stripes, marks of my fight to attain an identity of my own. I owe the person I am today to Martin's death. If he had not died, I am sure I would have lived happily ever after as a twentieth-century child wife never knowing what I was missing.

But today I am someone else. I am stronger, more independent. I have more understanding, more sympathy. A different perspective. I have a quiet love for Martin. I have passionate, poignant memories of him. He will always be part of me. But—

If I were to meet Martin today . . . ?

Would I love him?

I ask myself. Startled. What brought the question to my mind? I know. I ask it because I am a different woman.

Yes. Of course I would. I love him now. But Martin is dead. And I am a different woman. And the next time I love, if ever I do, it will be a different man, a different love.

Frightening.

But so is life. And wonderful.

Martin J. Caine
1920–1971

Martin's obituary never appeared in *The New York Times*. I was not able to pull myself together enough to write it, and I refused to let anyone else do it. Many of Martin's old friends were hurt; some were indignant. And I don't blame them. But most of all, I feel that I let Martin down. I'm sorry. It should have been in the paper for all the people who loved him.

Here it is. For Martin.

BALTIMORE, Md., May 13, 1971. Martin J. Caine, 50, a New York attorney, died today of cancer in the Marine Hospital (National Institutes of Health). He lived at 239 Central Park West. Mr. Caine, a graduate of New York University Law School, served with the Fifteenth Division of the United States Army Air Force during World War II and was decorated with the Silver Star for gallantry in action. An expert bridge player, he was a runner-up for the Reisinger Cup in 1959 and was a director of the Cavendish Club. He was a member of the New York State Bar Association and served on the Board of Governors of the Bankruptcy Bar Association. He leaves a son, Jonathan, 9, a daughter, Elizabeth, 5, and Lynn, his widow.